LANGUAGE A

Dorothy S. Stri[...]
Donna E. Alvermann and [...]
ADVISORY BOARD: Richard Allingto[...]
Anne Haas Dyson, Carole Edelsky, Mary Juzwik, Susan Lytle, Django Paris, Timothy Shanahan

MW01124808

Core Practices for Teaching Multilingual Students:
Humanizing Pedagogies for Equity
MEGAN MADIGAN PEERCY, JOHANNA M. TIGERT, &
DAISY E. FREDRICKS

Bringing Sports Culture to the English Classroom:
An Interest-Driven Approach to Literacy
Instruction
LUKE RODESILER

Culturally Sustaining Literacy Pedagogies:
Honoring Students' Heritages, Literacies, and
Languages
SUSAN CHAMBERS CANTRELL, DORIS WALKER-DALHOUSE,
& ALTHIER M. LAZAR, EDS.

Curating a Literacy Life:
Student-Centered Learning With Digital Media
WILLIAM KIST

Understanding the Transnational Lives and
Literacies of Immigrant Children
JUNGMIN KWON

The Administration and Supervision of Literacy
Programs, 6th Edition
SHELLEY B. WEPNER & DIANA J. QUATROCHE, EDS.

Writing the School House Blues: Literacy, Equity,
and Belonging in a Child's Early Schooling
ANNE HAAS DYSON

Playing With Language: Improving Elementary
Reading Through Metalinguistic Awareness
MARCY ZIPKE

Restorative Literacies:
Creating a Community of Care in Schools
DEBORAH L. WOLTER

Compose Our World: Project-Based Learning in
Secondary English Language Arts
ALISON G. BOARDMAN, ANTERO GARCIA, BRIDGET
DALTON, & JOSEPH L. POLMAN

Digitally Supported Disciplinary Literacy for
Diverse K–5 Classrooms
JAMIE COLWELL, AMY HUTCHISON,
& LINDSAY WOODWARD

The Reading Turn-Around with Emergent
Bilinguals:
A Five-Part Framework for Powerful Teaching and
Learning (Grades K-6)
AMANDA CLAUDIA WAGER, LANE W. CLARKE,
& GRACE ENRIQUEZ

Race, Justice, and Activism in Literacy Instruction
VALERIE KINLOCH, TANJA BURKHARD,
& CARLOTTA PENN, EDS.

Letting Go of Literary Whiteness:
Antiracist Literature Instruction for White Students
CARLIN BORSHEIM-BLACK
& SOPHIA TATIANA SARIGIANIDES

The Vulnerable Heart of Literacy:
Centering Trauma as Powerful Pedagogy
ELIZABETH DUTRO

Amplifying the Curriculum: Designing Quality
Learning Opportunities for English Learners
AÍDA WALQUI & GEORGE C. BUNCH, EDS.

Arts Integration in Diverse K–5 Classrooms:
Cultivating Literacy Skills and Conceptual
Understanding
LIANE BROUILLETTE

Translanguaging for Emergent Bilinguals: Inclusive
Teaching in the Linguistically Diverse Classroom
DANLING FU, XENIA HADJIOANNOU, & XIAODI ZHOU

Before Words: Wordless Picture Books and the
Development of Reading in Young Children
JUDITH T. LYSAKER

Seeing the Spectrum: Teaching English Language
Arts to Adolescents with Autism
ROBERT ROZEMA

A Think-Aloud Approach to Writing Assessment:
Analyzing Process and Product with Adolescent
Writers
SARAH W. BECK

"We've Been Doing It Your Way Long Enough":
Choosing the Culturally Relevant Classroom
JANICE BAINES, CARMEN TISDALE, & SUSI LONG

Summer Reading: Closing the Rich/Poor
Reading Achievement Gap, 2nd Edition
RICHARD L. ALLINGTON & ANNE McGILL-FRANZEN, EDS.

Educating for Empathy:
Literacy Learning and Civic Engagement
NICOLE MIRRA

Preparing English Learners for College and Career:
Lessons from Successful High Schools
MARÍA SANTOS ET AL.

Reading the Rainbow: LGBTQ-Inclusive Literacy
Instruction in the Elementary Classroom
CAITLIN L. RYAN & JILL M. HERMANN-WILMARTH

Educating Emergent Bilinguals: Policies, Programs,
and Practices for English Learners, 2nd Edition
OFELIA GARCÍA & JO ANNE KLEIFGEN

Social Justice Literacies in the English Classroom:
Teaching Practice in Action
ASHLEY S. BOYD

Remixing Multiliteracies: Theory and Practice from
New London to New Times
FRANK SERAFINI & ELISABETH GEE, EDS.

Culturally Sustaining Pedagogies: Teaching and
Learning for Justice in a Changing World
DJANGO PARIS & H. SAMY ALIM, EDS.

Choice and Agency in the Writing Workshop:
Developing Engaged Writers, Grades 4-6
FRED L. HAMEL

continued

For volumes in the NCRLL Collection (edited by JoBeth Allen and Donna E. Alvermann) and the Practitioners Bookshelf Series (edited by Celia Genishi and Donna E. Alvermann), as well as other titles in this series, please visit www.tcpress.com.

Language and Literacy Series, *continued*

Assessing Writing, Teaching Writers
MARY ANN SMITH & SHERRY SEALE SWAIN

The Teacher-Writer
CHRISTINE M. DAWSON

Every Young Child a Reader
SHARAN A. GIBSON & BARBARA MOSS

"You Gotta BE the Book," 3rd Edition
JEFFREY D. WILHELM

Personal Narrative, Revised
BRONWYN CLARE LAMAY

Inclusive Literacy Teachings
LORI HELMAN ET AL.

The Vocabulary Book, 2nd Edition
MICHAEL F. GRAVES

Reading, Writing, and Talk
MARIANA SOUTO-MANNING & JESSICA MARTELL

Go Be a Writer!
CANDACE R. KUBY & TARA GUTSHALL RUCKER

Partnering with Immigrant Communities
GERALD CAMPANO ET AL.

Teaching Outside the Box but Inside the Standards
BOB FECHO ET AL., EDS.

Literacy Leadership in Changing Schools
SHELLEY B. WEPNER ET AL.

Literacy Theory as Practice
LARA J. HANDSFIELD

Literacy and History in Action
THOMAS M. MCCANN ET AL.

Pose, Wobble, Flow
ANTERO GARCIA & CINDY O'DONNELL-ALLEN

Newsworthy—Cultivating Critical Thinkers, Readers, and Writers in Language Arts Classrooms
ED MADISON

Engaging Writers with Multigenre Research Projects
NANCY MACK

Teaching Transnational Youth— Literacy and Education in a Changing World
ALLISON SKERRETT

Uncommonly Good Ideas— Teaching Writing in the Common Core Era
SANDRA MURPHY & MARY ANN SMITH

The One-on-One Reading and Writing Conference
JENNIFER BERNE & SOPHIE C. DEGENER

Critical Encounters in Secondary English, 3rd Edition
DEBORAH APPLEMAN

Transforming Talk into Text—Argument Writing, Inquiry, and Discussion, Grades 6–12
THOMAS M. MCCANN

Reading and Representing Across the Content Areas
AMY ALEXANDRA WILSON & KATHRYN J. CHAVEZ

Writing and Teaching to Change the World
STEPHANIE JONES, ED.

Educating Literacy Teachers Online
LANE W. CLARKE & SUSAN WATTS-TAFFEE

WHAM! Teaching with Graphic Novels Across the Curriculum
WILLIAM G. BROZO ET AL.

Critical Literacy in the Early Childhood Classroom
CANDACE R. KUBY

Inspiring Dialogue
MARY M. JUZWIK ET AL.

Reading the Visual
FRANK SERAFINI

Race, Community, and Urban Schools
STUART GREENE

ReWRITING the Basics
ANNE HAAS DYSON

Writing Instruction That Works
ARTHUR N. APPLEBEE ET AL.

Literacy Playshop
KAREN E. WOHLWEND

Critical Media Pedagogy
ERNEST MORRELL ET AL.

A Search Past Silence
DAVID E. KIRKLAND

The ELL Writer
CHRISTINA ORTMEIER-HOOPER

Reading in a Participatory Culture
HENRY JENKINS ET AL., EDS.

Real World Writing for Secondary Students
JESSICA SINGER EARLY & MEREDITH DECOSTA

Teaching Vocabulary to English Language Learners
MICHAEL F. GRAVES ET AL.

Bridging Literacy and Equity
ALTHIER M. LAZAR ET AL.

"Trust Me! I Can Read"
SALLY LAMPING & DEAN WOODRING BLASE

Reading Time
CATHERINE COMPTON-LILLY

The Successful High School Writing Center
DAWN FELS & JENNIFER WELLS, EDS.

Interrupting Hate
MOLLIE V. BLACKBURN

Playing Their Way into Literacies
KAREN E. WOHLWEND

Teaching Literacy for Love and Wisdom
JEFFREY D. WILHELM & BRUCE NOVAK

Urban Literacies
VALERIE KINLOCH, ED.

Bedtime Stories and Book Reports
CATHERINE COMPTON-LILLY & STUART GREENE, EDS.

Envisioning Knowledge
JUDITH A. LANGER

Envisioning Literature, 2nd Edition
JUDITH A. LANGER

Artifactual Literacies
KATE PAHL & JENNIFER ROWSELL

Change Is Gonna Come
PATRICIA A. EDWARDS ET AL.

Harlem on Our Minds
VALERIE KINLOCH

Children, Language, and Literacy
CELIA GENISHI & ANNE HAAS DYSON

Children's Language
JUDITH WELLS LINDFORS

Storytime
LAWRENCE R. SIPE

Core Practices for Teaching Multilingual Students

Humanizing Pedagogies for Equity

Megan Madigan Peercy, Johanna M. Tigert,
and Daisy E. Fredricks

Foreword by Christian J. Faltis

TEACHERS COLLEGE PRESS

TEACHERS COLLEGE | COLUMBIA UNIVERSITY
NEW YORK AND LONDON

To my parents, Nancy and Dennis Madigan, and my children, Paige, Cole, and Rhys, who have been my most important teachers.

To my husband Brad, and my in-laws, Martha and Dave, for your unfailing support and love, always.

My deep gratitude to Mary Burbank and Linda Valli for being wonderful role models, mentors, and friends on my path to becoming and being a teacher educator and scholar.

In memory of my beloved grandmother, Genevieve M. Madigan, who was always so generous in supporting my education.

—MMP

Omistan tämän kirjan vanhemmilleni, jotka opettivat minulle jo varhain luki- ja kielitaidon merkityksen ja jaksoivat kuunnella lapsena kirjoittamiani tarinoita. Sanoin aina että minusta tulee isona kirjailija. En tosin arvannut että ensimmäinen kirjani olisi oppikirja eikä romaani.

—JMT

To my husband, Darien, and my children, August and Leif, who challenge and inspire me every day. Thank you for your patience and support on this journey. In loving memory of my grandparents, Herb and Wilma, for always believing in me. I hope I've made you proud.

—DEF

Published by Teachers College Press,® 1234 Amsterdam Avenue, New York, NY 10027

Copyright © 2022 by Teachers College, Columbia University

Front cover photos by Alexis Doty.

Library of Congress Cataloging-in-Publication Data

Names: Peercy, Megan Madigan, author. | Tigert, Johanna M., author. | Fredricks, Daisy E., author. | Faltis, Christian, 1950– writer of foreword.
Title: Core practices for teaching multilingual students : humanizing pedagogies for equity / Megan Madigan Peercy, Johanna M. Tigert, and Daisy E. Fredricks ; foreword by Christian J. Faltis.
Description: New York, NY : Teachers College Press, [2023] | Series: Language and literacy series | Includes bibliographical references and index.
Identifiers: LCCN 2022047030 (print) | LCCN 2022047031 (ebook) | ISBN 9780807768211 (hardcover ; acid-free paper) | ISBN 9780807768204 (paperback ; acid-free paper) | ISBN 9780807781654 (epub)
Subjects: LCSH: Multilingual education. | Multilingualism in children. | Holistic education. | Language arts—Correlation with content subjects. | LCGFT: Essays.
Classification: LCC LC3715 .P44 2023 (print) | LCC LC3715 (ebook) | DDC 370.117/5—dc23/eng/20221026
LC record available at https://lccn.loc.gov/2022047030
LC ebook record available at https://lccn.loc.gov/2022047031

ISBN 978-0-8077-6820-4 (paper)
ISBN 978-0-8077-6821-1 (hardcover)
ISBN 978-0-8077-8165-4 (ebook)

Printed on acid-free paper
Manufactured in the United States of America

Contents

Foreword   *Christian J. Faltis*   vii

Acknowledgments   xi

Introduction   1

1. Knowing Students   12

2. Building a Positive Learning Environment   27

3. Content and Language Instruction   43

4. Language and Literacy Development   61

5. Assessment   76

6. Relationships and Advocacy   94

7. Putting It All Together   111

8. Humanizing the Teaching Experience: Challenges and Solutions   127

Appendix   139

References   147

Index   157

About the Authors   163

Foreword

Early in my academic career, I learned that there was very little research or materials available for preparing teachers to teach students learning English who had entered school strong in another language. In the 1990s, I began to envision a book for teachers to learn pedagogical practices that I believed supported newcomers, English learners, and especially Spanish-speaking children and youth. I worked with Rudolfo Jacobson on developing the New Concurrent Approach (Jacobson & Faltis, 1991), a pedagogy that encouraged bilingual teachers and students to use code-switching in the classroom, now known more generally as translanguaging (García & Li Wei, 2014).

In 1993, the first edition of *Joinfostering: Adapting Teaching Strategies for the Multilingual Classroom* was published. The book's premise was to offer pedagogical practices to engage all students, and particularly English learners/multilingual students, so that they had equitable access to, participation in, and benefits from all classroom and school-based learning activities. Fast-forward now to this new book, *Core Practices for Teaching Multilingual Students,* and it is easy to see how far we have come. With the social and translanguaging turns in pedagogy, there are new understandings about multilingualism, language and literacy development for multilingual students, assessment practices, building socially and emotionally strong learning communities, and engaging with multilingual communities.

The three authors of this book are all former classroom teachers who have gone on to the academy to work tirelessly with teacher candidates seeking teaching certification for working in today's multilingual classrooms. I have read and learned a great deal from all the authors, but when I read the manuscript for this book, I realized there is much more to learn from them about critically conscious ways of preparing teachers for multilingual classrooms and schools.

This book uses a powerful humanizing approach comprised of six core practices for teaching multilingual students and connecting with their families. The humanizing approach for preparing teachers used in this book focuses on these practices, which enable all students, but especially racialized multilingual students, to experience educational equity, have their cultural and linguistic practices affirmed, and participate in and benefit from school in meaningful ways without fear, anxiety, or ridicule. Educators who use this book will learn to see their students as capable in bringing home knowledge to school settings and will learn ways to make this knowledge integral to classroom teaching and learning. The humanizing approach used in this book compels teachers to constantly disrupt harmful language ideologies and power dynamics, and advocate for developing students' critical consciousness while they experience schooling.

Indeed, there are core practices that all teachers should rehearse and enact during their coursework and field experiences, but what Megan Peercy, Johanna Tigert, and Daisy Fredricks advocate for and invite readers to learn are core practices (Peercy, 2014; Peercy et al., 2020) that are specifically designed for classrooms and schools to teach children who are learning English and to support their families in a manner that affirms educational dignity (Poza, 2021). The way this book is laid out—from getting to know your students and creating a positive learning environment, to addressing content and language learning and literacy development, building better assessments, infusing culturally and linguistically sustaining practices and materials, and creating strong bonds with the community, both as a teacher and an advocate—makes it an educational gem for teacher educators and teacher candidates who wish to move toward educational dignity for multilingual learners in schools and within systems that have been less than supportive of their cultural and linguistic practices.

What I find particularly appealing about this book is that it provides well-founded pedagogical practices that are connected to what is currently understood about language development, culturally and linguistically sustaining pedagogy, and parental and community involvement and advocacy. It also provides readers with real classroom examples of how classroom teachers integrate the core practices to engage with students across grade levels, and for the various vibrant assemblages of language that students are developing, from those who are at the beginning phrase in their new language to those who are expanding their language through literacy practices coupled with the display of their ideas (Bunch, 2014).

The authors provide a range of real classroom examples that offer ways to incorporate translanguaging and the use of students' home languages, even for teachers who do not speak or understand the home languages used by their students. For them, translanguaging can play a key role in eliciting and making sense of emergent bilingual students' ideas, and the ways they display their continually developing knowledge and ideas.

Teacher candidates who learn about teaching English learners from this book on core practices for multilingual learners will gain a clear vision of humanizing pedagogy. Readers will learn to engage in core practices of pedagogy that will make their teaching and their students' learning culturally and linguistically sustaining and rigorous, in ways that meet not only language and content learning goals, but also the socio-emotional needs of all students.

—*Christian J. Faltis*

REFERENCES

Bunch, G. C. (2014). The language of ideas and the language of display: Reconceptualizing "academic language" in linguistically diverse classrooms. *International Multilingual Research Journal, 8*(1), 70–86.

Faltis, C. (1993). *Joinfostering: Adapting teaching strategies for the multilingual classroom.* Macmillan.

García, O., & Wei, L. (2014). *Translanguaging: Language, bilingualism and education.* Palgrave Macmillan. https://doi.org/10.1057/9781137385765

Jacobson, R., & Faltis, C. (Eds.) (1991). *Language distribution issues in bilingual schooling.* Multilingual Matters Ltd.

Peercy, M. M. (2014). Challenges in enacting core practices in language teacher education: A self-study. *Studying Teacher Education, 10*(2), 146–162.

Peercy, M. M., Kidwell, T., Lawyer, M., Tigert, J., Fredricks, D., Feagin, K., & Stump, M. (2020). Experts at being novices: What new teachers can add to practice-based teacher education efforts. *Action in Teacher Education, 42*(3), 212–233. https://doi.org/10.1080/01626620.2019.1675201

Poza, L. E. (2021). Adding flesh to the bones: Dignity frames for English learner education. *Harvard Educational Review, 91*(4), 482–510. https://doi.org/10.17763/1943-5045-91.4.482

Acknowledgments

This book has been a labor of love. It emerged from our collective experiences teaching multilingual students, as well as working with pre-service and in-service teachers who were themselves teaching multilingual students, and considering the kinds of questions that educators raise about how to best serve students while also drawing on their tremendous resources. We had the good fortune of working, as their university supervisors and course instructors, with the group of pre-service and early career teachers featured in this book. They raised amazing questions about enacting humanizing practice, and we worked together for several years to generate a shared vision of the kinds of resources that might help teachers of multilingual students do so. In many ways, this book exists because of the questions and ideas offered by this group. We have been privileged to watch them grow as educators over the course of several years of collaboration, and we have grown along with them.

We would like to take this opportunity to express our tremendous gratitude to the teachers who appear in the pages of this book—Andrea, Andrew, Chris, Erica, Kendall, Lisa, Melissa, Nancy, Stephanie, and TC—as well as other teachers who do not get named in these chapters, but who spent so much time with us over several years as we co-developed a vision for humanizing core practices for multilingual students. Thank you for welcoming us into your classrooms; for discussing your questions, dilemmas, doubts, and successes in teaching; for trusting us and each other enough to be very honest about your practice; for your brilliant questions and ideas; for your extraordinary devotion to your students; and for your remarkable commitment to your growth and your colleagues' growth as professionals. We are also grateful to the administrators who welcomed us into their buildings, and to the students in these schools who are the reason we all do this work.

We also extend our sincere thanks to our teacher educator colleagues who have been part of the larger project from which this book emerged, including Dr. Tabitha Kidwell, Karen Feagin, Dr. Wyatt Hall, Megan DeStefano Lawyer, Dr. Megan Stump, Jennifer Himmel, Rebecca Ramirez, and Dr. Christina Budde. And our special thanks to doctoral student extraordinaire, Melanie Hardy, who has helped us in so many critically important ways to get this book to the finish line. We couldn't have done it without all of you.

Clearly, we haven't written this book alone. There were also important thought partners in this work as we developed our ideas and sought feedback. For serving in this important role, we want to thank Dr. Francis Troyan, Dr. Linda Valli, Dr. Nancy Dubetz, Dr. Manka Varghese, and many others who attended conference presentations about this work and asked us important questions as we developed our ideas.

Our thanks also to the Teachers College Press staff who have supported this project from its inception, and especially our editor, Emily Spangler. Gratitude also to the Spencer Foundation, whose funding helped make this work possible. The views expressed are those of the authors and do not necessarily reflect the views of the Spencer Foundation.

We are also indebted to our families who supported us and waited patiently as we wrote down "just one more thing" when inspiration struck.

Finally, we stand in awe of multilingual students and their families, and their remarkable resilience and assets. We hope that the ideas we share in this book make a positive contribution to what you experience in schools.

Introduction

> When I learn different techniques or strategies from my coursework, I think
> "Can I really apply this?" and "What does it really look like with my students?"
>
> —Lisa, secondary ESOL student teacher

The concerns expressed above by Lisa are not unusual for teachers as they enter a profession that is increasingly complex and demanding. One aspect of teaching that often leaves teachers feeling unprepared and unsupported is the growing number of multilingual students in U.S. classrooms today. These students include over five million officially designated English learners (ELs) (www.ncela.ed.gov) and millions of other students who speak languages other than English in their homes or communities but do not have an EL designation at school. These learners are often marginalized in schools because of their language backgrounds as well as their socioeconomic, racial/ethnic, cultural, religious, and immigrant backgrounds (Salazar, 2013; Sleeter & Zavala, 2020).

This book is based on a long-term collaborative research project that a team of teachers and teacher educators worked on together. The team included 13 novice elementary and secondary teachers of multilingual students, and eight teacher educators who supported the teachers as course instructors and university supervisors in the university program where they received their teacher licensure in teaching ESOL (English for Speakers of Other Languages). Our team wanted to find ways to make key practices for teaching multilingual students accessible to teachers from the beginning of their careers in the classroom.

Novice teachers—the majority of whom continue to come from White, middle-class, monolingual English-speaking backgrounds—struggle to bring together effective language and content teaching practices and socially just, culturally responsive pedagogies that are humanizing for their multilingual students and ensure equitable educational outcomes for them. We wanted to address the kinds of questions that Lisa asked about how to do the work of teaching her students, and how to do so in humanizing ways. In this book, we offer a framework for engaging in such work.

1

CORE PRACTICES FOR TEACHING MULTILINGUAL STUDENTS

In this book, we detail six core practices for teaching multilingual students through classroom examples. We believe these six practices can provide you with a clear understanding of how you can enact humanizing pedagogy with the vibrant, talented, growing number of multilingual students in schools. Core practices are different from wider arrays of best practices identified in other publications and materials for educators. They are defined as a small number of foundational practices that support student success and teacher growth and that can be learned in the very first years of teaching, and we identify them as providing support for enacting practice that aligns with a humanizing mindset.

Researchers have identified core practices for other content areas, including math, science, history, world languages, and English/language arts (Glisan & Donato, 2017; Grossman, 2018; McDonald et al., 2013; TeachingWorks, 2021; Windschitl et al., 2012). Here, we focus on practices that are useful in any content area but are targeted to identifying the resources and needs of multilingual students. We have found that teachers want assistance with how to teach multilingual students in humanizing and equitable ways, and hope that the core practices we identify here, and the classroom examples we provide, do just that. The examples of core practices that we share in this book come from the classrooms of ESOL specialists; however, we think these practices are beneficial for any teacher working with multilingual students. These are the six core practices we have identified for teaching multilingual students:

- Knowing students
- Building a positive learning environment
- Planning and enacting content and language instruction that meets students at their current level
- Supporting language and literacy development
- Assessing in ways that are attentive to students' language proficiency
- Developing positive relationships and advocating with and for colleagues, families, stakeholders, and yourself

We arrived at these practices through the collaborative efforts of our team over a period of several years. Through an iterative and participatory process, we eventually refined a set of core practices for teaching multilingual students that are grounded in observation, interview, artifact, and team meeting data (see Figure A.1 in the Additional Resources in the Appendix for a synthesized description of these practices). We share examples of these practices throughout this book. In doing so, we aim to help Lisa and other teachers of multilingual students answer the question: "What does that really look like in the classroom?"

Table I.1. Core Practices for Teaching Multilingual Students

1. *Knowing students* within the context of both school and their lives outside school, and integrating your knowledge of students':

- Home language and English language background
- Home language and English language literacy
- Prior schooling
- Interests
- Experiences at home and in community

2. *Building a positive learning environment* through:

- Consistent routines, high expectations, and procedures that support learning
- Culturally and linguistically responsive/sustaining pedagogy
- Development of students' social-emotional skills

3. *Planning and enacting content and language instruction* in ways that meet students at their current level through the use of:

- Comprehensible input
- Scaffolding
- Differentiation
- Integrated content and language objectives

4. Supporting *language and literacy development* by:

- Promoting vocabulary development
- Using students' home language knowledge as a resource
- Attending to and appropriately prioritizing receptive and productive language skills at the word, sentence, and discourse level
- Adapting instruction based on awareness of the complexity of language and students' language development needs

5. *Assessing* in ways that are attentive to students' language proficiency, including:

- Designing and using formal and informal assessments that match content and language objectives and approaches to instruction, and that measure content and language knowledge separately and fairly
- Interpreting standardized tests (including English language proficiency tests) and other formal assessments to design appropriate instruction for students
- Differentiating formal and informal assessment to match student abilities

6. Developing *positive relationships* with colleagues, families, stakeholders, and self by:

- Collaborating with and reciprocally sharing expertise with mainstream colleagues and other specialists
- Connecting with families to support students, families, and instruction
- Engaging in advocacy with colleagues, administrators, policymakers, and community to support student learning and social-emotional needs
- Practicing self-care for well-being

The purpose of using these core practices when teaching multilingual students is so that teachers like you can engage in rigorous and meaningful instruction that supports multilingual students in reaching their highest potential. Our hope is that these core practices help illustrate what practice with multilingual students can and should look like with an explicit commitment to equity. We feel it is critically important to connect these practices directly to humanizing aims to explicitly support novice teachers (hereafter NTs) of multilingual students, particularly because multilingual students are often minoritized in multiple ways. Each of these core practices is important for every learner, yet they all have dimensions that are specific to teaching multilingual students. In Chapters 1–7, we offer details that help illustrate what teachers of multilingual students can do to make each of the core practices come to life. For additional examples, please look at our video clips about humanizing core practices for multilingual students: https://education.umd.edu/edterps -learning-academy/resources.

It is also important to note, however, that the research in core practices has been criticized for marginalizing issues of equity and justice (Daniels & Varghese, 2020; Dutro & Cartun, 2016; Philip et al., 2019). Some scholars have argued that when we put practice at the center of our attention, we risk prescribing approaches to teaching that ignore the value of each student and marginalize equity by offering formulaic, rather than responsive, instruction to learners. However, we know from research that teachers need structured opportunities to engage in practice and reflection that leads to more than only an awareness of diversity (Lenski et al., 2005; Teemant, 2014; Young, 2010). Identifying concrete practices that support teachers' humanizing practice with multilingual students is one way to foster more equitable teaching.

WHAT IS HUMANIZING PEDAGOGY?

Humanizing pedagogy is foundational to teaching multilingual students in equitable ways. As such, it underpins each of the core practices subsequently described in Chapters 1–6 of this book. In general, humanizing pedagogy challenges the "education debt" (Ladson-Billings, 2006), or the "opportunity gap" (Carter & Welner, 2013) that exists for multilingual students. This debt, or gap, is the accrual of policies and experiences that limit access for multilingual students to the kinds of opportunities that White, middle-class, English-dominant students regularly have because the latter students' experiences are reflected in the curriculum, and because their speech and writing patterns, skin color, socioeconomic status, and home language are all privileged in school settings and the larger society.

We argue that humanizing pedagogy is a crucial way to address this opportunity gap, especially when teaching multilingual students. The many linguistic and cultural resources multilingual students bring with them to school are often not well understood by their teachers or their peers, who may have very different life experiences. Furthermore, multilingual students are frequently left on the margins of classrooms because teachers, though well-intentioned, do not feel well-prepared to teach them. Teachers often note that they are uncertain about how to teach in humanizing ways, even when they do hold humanizing mindsets.

We define humanizing pedagogy according to the following principles:

1. Humanizing pedagogy requires teachers to know their students as whole human beings. According to Carter Andrews and Castillo (2016), humanizing pedagogy is comprised of both mindsets and practices "that foster learning environments where the resources and needs of the whole student are considered," that "help students realize and enact more fully human identities," and that promote "inclusion in the classroom" (p. 113). Attending to the whole student includes considering their families, communities, home languages and cultures, socioeconomic circumstances, emotional well-being, and other factors that contribute to their identities.

2. Humanizing pedagogy values the assets and resources students bring to the classroom. Students thrive when their backgrounds, culture, and life experiences are valued in their educational settings and when their cultural and linguistic resources are acknowledged and capitalized on to improve teaching and learning (Salazar, 2010). Therefore, the humanization of teaching "requires educators to value the lived experiences, perspectives, and cultural knowledge young people bring with them into schools" (Kinloch, 2018, p. 14). Humanizing pedagogy means that students are valued both as individuals and as members of the classroom community.

3. Humanizing pedagogy is based on mutually caring, trusting relationships between teachers and students (Salazar, 2010). Humanizing relationships between teachers and students are "grounded in a discourse of care and compassion" (Kinloch, 2015, p. 31). Students should be understood as rich contributors to the classroom to fully benefit from classroom instruction and experience a supportive learning environment.

4. Humanizing pedagogy involves students as active participants in their own learning. It centers the student in all educational interactions. Citing Bartolomé (1994), Salazar (2013) argues that humanizing pedagogy positions "students as critically engaged, active participants in the co-construction of knowledge" (p. 128). Further, Kinloch (2015) explains that in humanizing pedagogy, knowledge is understood as reciprocal, co-constructed, and "rooted in mutual exchanges" (p. 31).

5. Humanizing pedagogy draws on students' experiences and knowledge. It is culturally and linguistically responsive and integrates students' sociocultural and linguistic resources into instructional practice. Humanizing pedagogy makes students' resources and perspectives integral to instruction (Bartolomé, 1994) and focuses on what students can do and achieve with their cultural and linguistic resources (Salazar, 2010). Therefore, humanizing pedagogy also strengthens students' ethnic and linguistic identities (Salazar, 2010).

6. Humanizing pedagogy is academically rigorous and meaningful. Humanizing teaching holds students to high expectations, expecting them to be "actively participating in class, working hard to produce high quality work, treating others with respect, and participating on [sic] complex cognitive tasks" (Siwatu et al., 2017, p. 866). In addition, humanizing pedagogy increases academic rigor through a focus on higher-order thinking skills (Salazar, 2010). This focus assists students in gaining knowledge and communication skills that are valued by society (Bartolomé, 1994).

7. Humanizing pedagogy responds to the particulars of each unique teaching context. Teachers who approach teaching through a humanizing lens recognize that students' experiences are shaped by their contexts. As Bartolomé (1994) reminds us, it is not the particular lesson or an activity that makes teaching and learning humanizing; rather, it is "the teacher's politically clear educational philosophy that underlies the varied methods and lessons/activities she or he employs that make the difference" (p. 179). Because all teaching contexts and the people within them have their particular variations, any framework—including that of the core practices we present in this book—will need to flexibly respond to those variations, while adhering to a clear vision of humanizing pedagogy.

8. Humanizing pedagogy disrupts traditional power dynamics in schools and classrooms. Carter Andrews and Castillo (2016) posit that teaching is humanizing when "power is shared by students and instructors" (p. 113). Further, Salazar (2010) argues that teachers who engage in humanizing their instruction challenge the role of educational institutions and educators in maintaining inequitable systems, advocate for innovative approaches to improve the education of all learners, and develop students' critical consciousness. Developing students' critical consciousness involves offering students opportunities to examine and question issues that impact them, with the goal of disrupting inequities. For instance, in one example of humanizing practice, a teacher and her 1st-grade students challenged traditional power dynamics by exploring why

certain students were pulled out of class for instruction during the school day, while others were not, and whether there were similar inequities at play in pull-out instruction and in other examples of segregation (Souto-Manning, 2010).

NOTE ON TERMINOLOGY

School systems often use the term English language learners (ELLs) or the U.S. federal designation, English learners (ELs). However, we use the term "multilingual students" throughout this book as a wide umbrella for students with many different language backgrounds, such as students new to both English and the United States, students who were born in the United States and exposed to English throughout their childhood but designated as ELs when they enter school, and students who may have learned multiple languages throughout their childhood as a result of their life experiences (García & Kleifgen, 2010). By positioning students as multilingual, we draw from an asset-based orientation that focuses on their rich multilingual abilities and the potential inherent in encouraging the maintenance and further development of their home languages alongside English language and literacy.

ORGANIZATION OF THIS BOOK

The chapters that follow explore each of the six core practices we have identified and provide examples of them. Chapter 1 examines five ways teachers can integrate knowledge of the following about students in practice when teaching multilingual students:

- Home language and English language background
- Home language and English language literacy
- Prior schooling
- Interests
- Experiences at home and in their communities

This knowledge is particularly important when teaching multilingual students because the majority of teachers in U.S. PK–12 classrooms do not share linguistic, cultural, socioeconomic, and other demographic aspects with their multilingual students. Many do not live in their students' communities, speak another language, or have experience with different language and literacy systems. Learning about students and integrating this knowledge into their practice helps teachers to better plan, teach, and assess their students. It also helps teachers to understand their students as complete human beings who bring a rich, full repertoire of experiences and knowledge to the classroom.

In Chapter 2, we examine how teachers can build a positive learning environment for multilingual students, who have more frequently experienced trauma, interrupted schooling, and linguistic and cultural incongruence between their experiences and the norms of U.S. schools. Specific ways for teachers to build a positive classroom environment to support multilingual students both academically and emotionally include the following:

- Clear procedures, consistent routines, and high expectations
- The use of culturally and linguistically responsive and sustaining pedagogy
- Developing students' social-emotional skills

To engage in this core practice means that teachers need to carefully consider how language, culture, and prior experiences impact multilingual students, and how classroom spaces, routines, and expectations can be rethought and reorganized to ensure students are academically successful and emotionally safe. This is especially important for multilingual students, who may still be in the process of acquiring the linguistic and cultural frames for understanding their new classroom environments. Enacting this core practice also means that teachers reconsider rigid, behavioristic, and punitive disciplinary actions that are often offered as a solution for teachers to "control" classrooms populated by multilingual students.

Because integration of content and language learning are a critical aspect of instruction for multilingual students, this requires teachers' careful attention. In Chapter 3, classroom pedagogy is our focus as we explore four ways teachers can plan and enact content and language instruction that meet multilingual students at their current level and challenge them to keep growing in their content and language knowledge. These include their use of the following:

- Comprehensible input
- Scaffolding
- Differentiation
- Clear and integrated content and language objectives

While these aspects of teaching can benefit every student, each requires teachers' careful attention to language as they consider how to best plan and teach their lessons. These aspects involve creating links between new concepts and supports (through visuals, gestures, and other means) that make the new language transparent, carefully providing and then removing linguistic supports as they are no longer needed, and creating tasks with varying linguistic complexity depending on learners' language levels. Building these features into instruction brings together content instruction with appropriate support for simultaneous language learning, creating the possibility for rigorous, meaningful, age-appropriate instruction that challenges students and positions them as active participants in the learning process.

In Chapter 4, we consider how teachers can support language and literacy development for multilingual students. Language and literacy are fundamental building blocks to learning in all the content areas and provide keys to much of what students need for success in and beyond school. These building blocks are particularly critical for multilingual students who have a wealth of linguistics resources in their home languages. However, multilingual students need assistance with leveraging their existing language and literacy abilities while developing their growing abilities in English. We highlight four ways teachers can enact this:

- Promoting vocabulary development
- Using students' home languages as a resource
- Attending to both receptive (listening and reading) and productive (speaking and writing) language use in the use of words, sentences, and more extended discourse
- Adapting instruction based on the complexity of language

When teachers are aware that language and literacy development go much deeper than learning individual words, and that multilingual students' existing linguistic resources can be used in additive ways, they can provide rigorous, asset-oriented pedagogy that is underpinned by a deep understanding of language.

In Chapter 5, we explore how assessment, while important for all learners, differs when teaching multilingual students. Frequently, assessments are given in English, even to students who do not yet speak English! This is appropriate when trying to determine students' proficiency in English, but not at all effective when the aim is to understand students' content knowledge, or their literacy skills in their home languages, for instance. Language and content need to be decoupled from one another in assessments, and this can be challenging for teachers to do. In this chapter, we highlight three considerations for enacting meaningful assessments with multilingual students:

- Designing and using both formal and informal assessments for language and content
- Interpreting the results of standardized tests, including English language proficiency tests
- Differentiating formal and informal assessments appropriate for students' language development and content knowledge

When teachers know how to design appropriately challenging assessment that draws on students' assets, they are able to hold high standards and maintain rigor, which are important for students' full engagement in school.

In Chapter 6, we move from the classroom to a broader level, and consider ways teachers can develop positive relationships that support multilingual students:

- Collaborating with colleagues
- Making meaningful connections with families
- Engaging in advocacy with a variety of stakeholders (including administrators, policymakers, and the community)
- Practicing teacher self-care in a particularly demanding field in education

Strong relationships with a variety of stakeholders are needed because they create an informed and committed community of support around multilingual students and their teachers—in their classrooms, schools, communities, and in the policy arena. Strong collaborative relationships between teachers and families, as well as advocacy efforts on behalf of multilingual students, help contribute to awareness that they are often underserved, and make it possible to connect resources to multilingual students. Because the demands of working with underserved populations are high, teachers of multilingual students also need to regularly take time to care for themselves. When teachers engage in self-care, their happier and calmer demeanor positively impacts their students' moods and actions, making for a more humanizing learning environment for everyone.

In Chapter 7, we look across these six core practices and the ways they can be enacted to consider how each of them can help to humanize practice with multilingual students, who represent both a very vulnerable and promising population for our future. In this chapter, we share additional examples from teachers' practice for you to analyze and consider, and some tools to help you examine your own practice.

In Chapter 8, we share thoughts from the teachers and teacher educators involved in this project regarding what we learned from doing this work together. Recognizing that reflection is a key part of educator development, we share our own reflections in this chapter by both looking back at our work together and looking forward to what this means for our classrooms and for the field.

In closing, we want to emphasize that just as humanizing pedagogy is context-specific, situated in a particular time and place, with particular learners, so too are the core practices our team has identified in the hopes of supporting other teachers. The practices we share here emerged from our collaboration in a particular context and during a particular time. These practices are intended for your reflection on your work as you grow as a teacher, and they are not intended to be evaluative nor fixed in place. They must continue to be living ideas that inform your work as a teacher, as you bring your own set of experiences to your particular learners, in your particular settings.

QUESTIONS FOR REFLECTION

1. How would you define humanizing pedagogy in your own words?
2. Can you think of an example of seeing a teacher engage in humanizing pedagogy? What did the teacher do to humanize their pedagogy? How did students respond to this?
3. Of the six core practices highlighted in this chapter, which practices are you most interested in further exploring? Why?

CHAPTER 1

Knowing Students

> The teachers who really impacted me took the time to get to know me. Taking the time to talk to your students about where they come from, about the languages that they speak, the way they learn those languages, and their interests and motivations for learning that second language are really important because it'll help frame your relationship building with them, and also your lesson planning.
>
> —Nancy, secondary ESOL teacher

As Nancy explains above, knowing your students is fundamentally important for planning responsive instruction and for humanizing your practice. The teachers in our group described knowing students as the bedrock of all other practices they used in their classrooms, with both academic and affective dimensions. Knowing students is built through warm and respectful relationships and developed through acts such as greeting students each morning with enthusiasm, conducting brief check-ins, and taking time to learn about their families, home lives, and communities.

Through our collaboration, we found that teachers knew about their students in at least five different ways:

- Home language and English language background
- Home language and English language literacy
- Prior schooling
- Interests
- Experiences at home and in their communities

DIMENSIONS OF KNOWING MULTILINGUAL STUDENTS

Because humanizing practice involves all class members—students and teachers alike—being fully seen and appreciated for who they are, it is clear that knowing students is central to teachers' work. Research shows that teachers who have strong connections with their students demonstrate higher levels of student achievement, provide stronger supports for learner development, and experience a better sense of well-being themselves (e.g., Hamre & Pianta,

2006; Jennings & Greenberg, 2009; Spilt et al., 2011; Wubbels & Brekelmans, 2005). Furthermore, when teachers know their students well, they are better equipped to plan and enact instruction and assessment that are appropriately challenging, engaging, and motivating, as well as equity- and justice-oriented (Athanases & De Oliveira, 2008; Souto-Manning, 2010). Knowing about the backgrounds of all your students is clearly important; however, there are some dimensions of knowing students that are unique to the teaching of multilingual learners, and we want to highlight them here.

Home Language and English Language Background

Because it is important for multilingual students' overall development to gain skills in English while also sustaining and enhancing their home languages, teachers must combat the continued marginalization and devaluing of students' linguistic assets by U.S. schools. In the past, this marginalization often meant that multilingual students were forbidden to use anything other than English in schools, which not only robbed them of an important learning tool, but also dehumanized them by diminishing their linguistic identities to just "English learners." Today, an outright ban on home languages is less common, but the overwhelming presence of English in instruction and assessment itself sends multilingual students a clear message. Overlooking or devaluing students' home languages can be very damaging. As Chicana scholar Gloria Anzaldúa (1987) put it, "I am my language. Until I can take pride in my language, I cannot take pride in myself" (p. 59). Fortunately, educators are increasingly understanding the value of students' home languages.

The first step is to learn what language or languages your multilingual students speak in their homes and communities and what your students' proficiency in those languages is like. For example, some students may speak and comprehend the language well, but may not necessarily have strong literacy (reading and writing) skills in the language. Many schools today use a home language survey to uncover this information—this can be either a paper form or a short interview with the student or their family member. Some school districts even give students a home language assessment, if available in their language. It is also helpful to learn to speak even a few words of your students' home languages, such as greetings, and to know how these languages are similar to and different from English. Some ways to easily learn basic phrases and compare students' home languages with English include looking up that information online and asking the students themselves.

When you have some knowledge of students' home languages you can use the knowledge to do the following:

- Strategically use key vocabulary including cognates (words that look and sound similar and have the same meaning in the home language and English)

- Clarify words, grammatical forms, or instructions you know may be confusing for speakers of certain languages
- Give feedback and praise using students' home languages
- Use greetings, check-ins, and expressions of care and concern in students' home languages

These and other means of building rapport in students' home languages all go a long way in helping you know your students better. As we will see in this chapter, even when teachers do not speak students' home languages, they can ask students to teach them key words and aspects of the language that can be used instructionally for both academic and affective support. Furthermore, teachers' knowledge of what their students already have studied in English, and what their English language proficiency is, will help them to effectively reach students, challenge them, and target instruction in ways that are appropriate for students' existing English language abilities.

When we talk about language proficiency, we generally describe it as different levels of language ability. These levels can be as simple as newcomer, beginning, intermediate, and advanced language proficiency in listening, speaking, reading, and writing, or can involve categories that are identified through language proficiency testing. The teachers on our team all described their students' English skills as ranging across six levels (entering, emerging, developing, expanding, bridging, reaching) as measured by the WIDA ACCESS proficiency test (Chapter 5 will discuss WIDA ACCESS and other language proficiency assessments further). It is important to know that students can be at different levels of proficiency in each of the main language domains (listening, speaking, reading, and writing). Awareness of the ways in which multilingual students use each domain helps teachers to select materials, plan instruction, and support and assess learning (see, for instance, https://wida .wisc.edu/teach/can-do/descriptors). Kendall, an elementary ESOL teacher, explained that knowing about her students' language background helps her to provide more linguistically responsive instruction to her elementary students, and she gathers this knowledge in a variety of ways:

> We can get their enrollment file about their first language and their overall ESOL level and individual domain scores. Even if their overall level is intermediate, they might be higher in writing, and lower in reading, for instance. Being able to look at their individual domain scores gives me a clearer picture of my students. A lot of times their ESOL level doesn't actually seem to line up very nicely with their true proficiency. So, getting some anecdotal evidence from talking to them and talking to other teachers is really important for grouping purposes and for making sure that you're differentiating appropriately and creating engaging activities for them. Try to get them to talk as much as they can. If you ask them about things that they're excited

about, they're going to want to jump in and they're going to want to say as much as they can. And that's a really good way to gauge their proficiency.

Home Language and English Language Literacy

Since multilingual students' content area knowledge is most often assessed through reading and writing in English, it is especially important to be well informed about students' literacy skills. When you know about the ways in which students use their home languages for reading and writing, and the impact that students' home languages have on their understanding of the way print works, this can help teachers to support students' learning of print literacy in English. Differences between English and a student's home language may impact their understanding of the English alphabet; the connections they make among print, sounds, and meaning; and their understanding of the directionality of text. For instance, in Arabic, Hebrew, Urdu, and several other languages, text directionality is from right to left. These and other languages such as Chinese, Japanese, Korean, Russian, Ukrainian, and Burmese all use writing systems that are different from English.

Furthermore, teachers who know something about students' home language literacy know that students already understand the process of reading and that print carries meaning (also called print awareness). Thus, students who have some level of literacy in their home language know that written language works as a system to convey meaning, and that they need to learn the alphabet (print and cursive), pronunciation, vocabulary, and grammar that allow them to access and produce meaning in the new language. This is quite different from students who do not have prior literacy experience in their home languages and are learning principles of literacy for the first time. When you know that students have literacy abilities in their home languages, you understand that students don't need basic instruction in the principles of literacy. Instead, you can dive in and teach letter-sound combinations and syllable and word types in English and quickly begin using those words to introduce vocabulary in English, connecting that to vocabulary in students' home languages when possible (August & Shanahan, 2006; Snow et al., 2005; Vadasy & Nelson, 2012).

Additionally, you should know about the English literacy levels of your students. If you know about students' reading and writing abilities in English, you can better select, create, or modify appropriate texts for reading, as well as decide how much writing support to provide students. For instance, your students may need sentence starters, sentence stems, vocabulary banks, and other scaffolds depending on their English literacy level (for more on scaffolding your instruction, see Chapter 3). It is very different to require students to fill in blanks in already composed sentences with the aid of a word bank versus create new sentences on their own.

Language proficiency tests will provide you with some information about your multilingual students' reading and writing proficiency, but what the results say and how your students perform on literacy tasks in the classroom may differ because of test conditions, student anxiety, or other reasons. Many teachers also use less formal measures to get a sense of their multilingual students' reading and writing proficiency in their home languages and in English, including asking students to read a short passage to them, or to write down something about themselves.

For instance, Erica, an elementary ESOL teacher, noted that when she has multilingual students in her class who speak a home language with an alphabet similar to English (such as Spanish), she might ask them to read a passage in English aloud to her to see if they understand how to sound words out and decode text, even if they do not know English pronunciation or understand the meaning of what they are reading. This quick check allows her to determine whether her students already understand literacy practices in their home language, which means she can use that foundation to teach students to use those same literacy skills in English. Students' existing literacy abilities in English will determine what is most appropriate for challenging, yet adequately supported instruction. We focus on literacy instruction in more detail in Chapter 4.

Prior Schooling

Also fundamental to knowing your multilingual students is seeking information about their prior schooling. While it is important to know about the background knowledge and experiences of any new student, it is particularly critical when teaching multilingual students because their home and schooling experiences are frequently different from those their teachers and English-dominant classmates have had. Being informed about your students' prior schooling experiences helps you to make the most appropriate academic, cultural, linguistic, and affective bridges among the school, students, and their families.

It surprises many people new to working with multilingual students to learn that the majority of multilingual students enrolled in U.S. schools are actually born in the United States (Zong & Batalova, 2015). However, they may not have lived continuously in the United States, and their schooling may have involved frequent moves and inconsistent language programming (Menken & Kleyn, 2009). Multilingual students born in other countries may also have experienced inconsistent or interrupted schooling, as in the case of the high numbers of students who seek refuge in the United States each year (DHS, n.d.). Additionally, students who have been in school in refugee camps in other countries may have vastly different experiences of learning in those situations. Students who have experienced interrupted education or have not had formal education due to war and other challenging circumstances are often referred to as students with limited or interrupted formal education (SLIFE).

Furthermore, multilingual students may also have schooling experiences in their home countries that include very different school curricula, classroom expectations, school calendars, length of school days, class sizes, relationships with teachers, and expectations of family involvement, among many other potential factors. Questions pertaining to these factors can be incorporated into the home language survey, as well as uncovered informally by interacting with students and their families.

It is also important for teachers to know whether and for how long multilingual students have had an official "English learner" designation (determined by the school system's English language proficiency test, such as WIDA ACCESS). Those students who have been in U.S. schools for more than six years and who continue to qualify for language support services in English provided by the school system are considered long-term English learners (LTELs). An estimated 60% of students who are designated as EL in U.S. secondary schools are considered LTELs, and this number is continuing to grow (WestEd, 2016).

According to Menken and Kleyn (2009), students designated as LTELs are "often orally bilingual and sound like native English speakers. However, they typically have limited literacy skills in their native language, and their academic literacy skills in English are not as well developed as their oral skills are" (p. 26). Because they often perform below grade level in reading and writing, they struggle with literacy demands in all content areas. Their academic needs are therefore quite different than those of newly arrived ELs, which is a problem because ESOL curricula are typically targeted at new arrivals, particularly at the secondary level (Menken & Kleyn, 2009). Furthermore, students designated as LTELs tend to experience low graduation rates and may have a negative self-image as students because of the stigma attached to receiving language support (Dabach, 2014).

Interests and Experiences at Home and in Their Communities

The final two dimensions of knowing students that we want to highlight in this chapter are knowing students' interests and knowing about students' experiences at home and in their communities. While it is important for teachers of *all* learners to know about and integrate students' interests and their experiences at home and in their communities into the classroom, integration of this knowledge takes on a particular importance when teaching multilingual students. Because multilingual students are often from minoritized[1] groups, and they are frequently marginalized within their school settings, their interests and experiences at home and in their communities are not regularly known about or recognized.

Additionally, multilingual students may not take part in the kind of experiences that most White, middle-class, English-dominant speakers regularly have (e.g., Au, 1980; Heath, 1983; Michaels, 1981). Teachers of multilingual students, who are often from these dominant groups themselves, must take extra care not to make assumptions about the interests and experiences of multilingual students. They must instead find out about the kinds of interests and experiential resources their students bring to the classroom, and leverage and highlight them as ways to respect students and their families and to support their learning. Doing so helps students to feel seen as valued members of the classroom community, fosters student motivation and engagement, and supports their language development by allowing them to practice language with topics that are familiar to them. For instance, incorporation of home country or community geography, architecture, historical events, and other features that are familiar to multilingual students, which may not usually be highlighted in school materials or curricula, goes a long way in piquing student interest and making students feel valued in their classes, while also broadening the cultural and linguistic horizons and sensitivities of their peers. Chris, a secondary ESOL teacher, explained that he chose a picture of a place in Guatemala for a warm-up activity in his class because he thought that some students in his class would recognize it, and this sparked further conversation because of the personal connection they had to it: "I had a picture of San Pablo, Guatemala displayed and a couple of the Guatemalan kids in my class said, 'Oh, I know that lake!' and we talked about it after I put up the picture. I knew there were going to be some kids who recognized it and had something to say."

TC, a secondary ESOL science teacher, shared that she needs to know what students were experiencing outside the classroom so that she can support them in not just content learning but in understanding other circumstances that might be influencing their learning:

> If I don't know that's what's going on in their lives, if I'm constantly pushing, "Learn this," they're not going to be able to grasp what I'm trying to teach them because they have so many other worries at home. So it's super important to build a rapport and have that positive environment where they can share what's going on with me. It's a big problem with students in general, coming to school, feeling invisible. They come in and they're surrounded by all of these educators who are trying to teach them all the subjects, but they don't know anything about who they really are. So building that type of relationship is super important to me.

SEEING IT IN ACTION

It is important to note that knowing students is one of the less observable core practices. Although it is easy to see it manifested through warm relationships, a welcoming atmosphere, and well-planned, responsive lessons, each of the parts that comprise getting to know students and integrating that knowledge of students often happen in small moments in the classroom or outside regular instructional time. As Erica shared:

> My use of the "knowing students" core practice is not very evident simply from watching the lesson. In my experience, it is often the case that this core practice would not be evident to an outside observer. However, it is extremely important to enact this practice when planning because otherwise scaffolding and academic language development won't be accurately targeted.

Despite this challenge, we found many instances when it was clear that teachers knew their students well, and actively worked to learn about their students in a variety of ways.

Below we highlight examples from Kendall, Stephanie, and TC's ESOL classrooms. These examples illustrate how each of the teachers take opportunities to get to know their students and to use that knowledge to support both their academic instruction and their affective support of students. They humanize their pedagogy by making their students valued and essential members of their classroom community who bring important expertise to their whole class. They use students' home languages to build comprehension and community, draw upon students' interests and experiences to contextualize and ground new content and ideas, and actively use what they know about students' prior schooling and their literacy in their home language(s) and in English to create meaningful, connected, cohesive instruction.

Kendall

Kendall is an elementary ESOL teacher, teaching 2nd- and 3rd-grade pull-out and plug-in[2] lessons. In this example, she is teaching four lively 3rd-graders in a pull-out lesson on compare and contrast for her 3rd-grade students. She shared:

> They often write full sentences inside the Venn diagram, which means they get fewer ideas and have run out of steam before they get to the actual writing. In this lesson, students learn how to quickly and effectively complete a Venn diagram. In the following lessons, they will use key compare and contrast vocabulary to compose individual sentences and, finally, a paragraph.

Pay attention to how Kendall draws on her knowledge of students' *prior schooling* and their *interests* in her lesson.

> Kendall begins her lesson with the four intermediate-level students by showing them a picture of a Venn diagram and asking them to talk in

pairs about three questions: "What is this called? When do you use it? What do you write in it?" After a brief conversation in their pairs, Kendall and her students discuss their ideas. She tells the class that they will work together as a class to use a Venn diagram to compare and contrast two food items or two animals. To students' gasps of delight and enthusiasm, she suggests Takis (a spicy tortilla chip snack much loved by the elementary students in her school) as one of the food items, telling her students, "You guys are Taki experts." Kendall's students agree and suggest that they compare and contrast Takis with Doritos. After an animated conversation, Kendall and her 3rd-graders arrive at a shared understanding that the middle section of a Venn diagram contains the similarities in what is being compared and contrasted, and the left and right sections contain the differences.

Later, Kendall explained why she had chosen Doritos and Takis as the class example: "It is important for students to have many opportunities to share with each other and the group, and I try to choose topics that interest them. I also encourage them to think of themselves as experts and writers."

Kendall knew that her students were often asked to fill out Venn diagrams in their English language arts (ELA) class, but she had observed that they did not do so very effectively, writing long sentences rather than brief key ideas in the diagrams. She also knew that her students needed scaffolding with a graphic organizer to write a compare and contrast paragraph, a common text structure they would frequently need to produce. Therefore, Kendall created this set of lessons to help her students more effectively use a Venn diagram. Furthermore, Kendall knew that her students loved Takis and used this knowledge to have students write about a familiar and exciting topic to help enliven their understanding and use of Venn diagrams. Offering students a chance to write about something familiar positioned them as both experts and good writers.

In these lessons, Kendall was using both her knowledge of her students' prior schooling (that they struggled to use a common graphic organizer effectively to support their writing) and their interests (in Takis) to build her compare and contrast lesson. Her practice was humanizing because she centered students' knowledge and experiences with (and love for) Takis, making it possible for them to be expert contributors to the lesson. She clearly knew her students well, and valued their expertise, using her wider knowledge of her students to create a meaningful and engaging lesson for her 3rd-graders.

Stephanie

Like Kendall, Stephanie is an elementary ESOL teacher who teaches both plug-in and pull-out lessons. In this example, she demonstrates her awareness of students' home language and English language backgrounds and their prior schooling when she supports their understanding of a new word and draws upon students' experiences of being new somewhere.

Stephanie works on a lesson on inferencing with six students with intermediate proficiency in English at a table at the back of their 3rd-grade classroom. The objective on the board says, "Students will write an inference using a picture." There is also a statement written on the board that defines inferences: "What I see and read+what I know=What I infer about the characters." After a student reads the objective aloud, Stephanie begins the lesson by showing a picture of a new student, Sophia, meeting other students. The students in this picture are smiling and wearing orange backpacks. Stephanie starts the conversation about inferencing by sharing an example on a card that is not an inference, that says, "NOT AN INFERENCE: The students all have orange backpacks. The students are smiling." Then, Stephanie shares an example on another card that says, "INFERENCE: I infer the students are friendly and kind because they are smiling and welcoming to Sophia."

Stephanie: (Asks one of the students.) Can you tell me what key words we saw?

Nicholas: Friendly, kind, welcoming, smiling, students.

Stephanie: So, they said "Welcome," they were being welcoming. They were smiling, that's what we saw. Does it say anywhere on this picture, "We are friendly"?

Students: No.

Stephanie: Do you see the word *friendly*?

Students: No.

Stephanie: Do you see the word *kind*?

Students: No.

Stephanie: We were able to infer from our picture and our words that they were being friendly and kind. Has anybody ever been a new student in school?

Cassandra: Yes.

Stephanie: Cassandra, what does it feel like when you're the new student?

Cassandra: Shy.

Stephanie: Nicholas?

Nicholas: I felt, like, shy, nervous, and kind of mad.

Stephanie: Shy, nervous, and kind of mad? So, when somebody smiles at you, how do you feel? When you're the new student and somebody smiles at you? Adam, how do you feel?

Adam: I feel happy but when I was at the first day of school to Miss Frederick's class, I was nervous and shy because everyone, I don't know them, and on the next day, I was feeling less nervous and feeling happy.

Stephanie: Mm-hmm. When people start smiling and say, "Come sit with us," do you feel better?

Adam: Yeah.

Stephanie: And how do you think of those people? Do you think of them as kind people, or unkind people?

Students: Kind!

Stephanie: Do you think of them as friendly people, or unfriendly?

Students: Friendly.

Stephanie: So we just made one inference together.

After her lesson, Stephanie explained that she was using what she knew about her students to create topics for their inferencing activity: "I was trying to connect the content to things that they would be comfortable talking about anyway. A lot of them have the experience of being the new student."

In her lesson, Stephanie used students' prior experiences of being new somewhere to create a shared understanding of the content, in this case making inferences. Stephanie knew that understanding and using the word "inference" would be challenging for her multilingual students, which shows she was cognizant of the students' home language and English language backgrounds. However, Stephanie's example focused on a relatable experience and the emotions connected to it, which helped make the concept more concrete for her students. Students were engaged with the lesson and interested in sharing their own experiences of being the new student.

Choosing the topic of being new to a school also demonstrated that Stephanie was knowledgeable about students' prior schooling. She anticipated that many of her students had experiences of being the new student, and the conversation she had with her students not only served the purpose of teaching students the academic concept of an inference but also helped her learn even more about her students. Therefore, using this example in her lesson helped her continue to build a classroom community that was trusting and caring.

Like Kendall, Stephanie humanized her practice by using students' experiences to develop a meaningful lesson that was rigorous and engaging, while drawing on students as experts. She made their experiences central to a lesson on drawing inferences that could have easily used a set of examples much less familiar to them, and she normalized and made visible students' experiences of being new and feeling out of place, making it more acceptable to share those uncomfortable feelings in her classroom.

TC

TC is a secondary ESOL science teacher. In this example from TC's classroom, note how she values students' home languages, seeks information about their home language and English language literacy, and learns about their experiences and interests.

TC greets students as they arrive at her ESOL Science class for 9th-
and 10th-grade students. She stops to talk to two new students, Nelson
and Aliyah, who have recently come to the United States and have just
been enrolled in her class. She lets them know how to put the header
on their warm-up (name, date, class period) and that she will help them
throughout the class period. TC directs the class to get started on their
warm-up question ("How can we use a ruler?") for a lesson on mea-
surement. She begins the lesson with a discussion about using a ruler
to measure length, width, and height, and sprinkles key vocabulary in
Spanish and Russian (the home languages of the students in her class)
throughout the lesson.

TC: How do you say ruler?
Spanish-speaking students: Regla [ruler].
TC: Regla. (To Tanya, a Russian-speaking student.) How do you say
    ruler in Russian?
Tanya: Lineika.
TC: Lineika. Everybody. (Prompting class to repeat it.)
Students: Lineika.
TC: So how can we use a ruler? I want to hear from you because you
    know some of this vocabulary.
Adrian: ¡Medir! [To measure!]
TC: Medir. How do you say that in English?
Students: Measure.
TC: Measure. Everybody repeat: Measure.
Students: Measure.
TC: (Prompting one of the new students to repeat after her.) Nelson:
    Measure.
Nelson: Measure.
TC: Perfect, thank you. (Prompting the other new student to repeat after
    her.) Aliyah: Measure.
Aliyah: Measure.
TC: Thank you. Okay, so we always repeat, new students.

At the end of the class, TC asks for three student volunteers to model how to
introduce themselves to the class, stating their names, what language(s) they
speak, and one thing they like, each followed by applause and "Welcome!"
from the class. Next, she asks Nelson and Aliyah to follow that model and introduce themselves to the class, and they are greeted by their new classmates.

After her lesson, TC explained her reason for using classroom introductions
each time new students joined the class: "It makes them know that I know
them. I know what is going on in everybody's life, no matter how big my classes
are. That's definitely a big thing, because once you lose them, it's kind of hard

to bring them back in without seeming inauthentic. Like I can say, 'How's your dad doing?' because I know about them."

TC also shared why she used Russian in her class, where Tanya was the sole Russian speaker:

> When Tanya joined our class, nobody wanted to be in her group because this was during the first couple of weeks of school so the other Spanish-speaking students only wanted to speak Spanish to each other and they're like, "She doesn't understand me!" So I was like, "Let's learn some of her words." So we all learned some phrases in Russian like *hello, goodbye, thank you.* Tanya loved it, and she feels a lot more comfortable now. Because at first, she was not talking.

TC explained getting to know more about Tanya:

> If you're going to stereotype, you're automatically going to think, "Oh, she's well-to-do, she doesn't have any problems, and she can speak English almost fluently, we don't have to focus on her," but no! She was struggling! She didn't have any friends, nobody wanted to be her friend. If I asked her how she was doing, she clammed up. But then I got to know her, and then she comes up in the hall and says, "Can you help me with this?" So just making them feel more comfortable makes them open up in the classroom. I really think that they need to know that somebody has their back. Because without that they're not going to learn.

TC brought a number of dimensions of knowing students to her practice in the examples above. She clearly learned about, valued, and integrated students' home languages, and sought information about their home language and English language literacy, and about their experiences and interests outside school, beginning with their introductions of themselves to the class.

TC also shared how important it was for her to research information about her students' literacy levels so that she could appropriately support them in her class, describing how she consulted with other teachers and with counselors about students' literacy in their home languages and in English. In Tanya's case, she was aware that she had a high level of proficiency in English, and that she needed emotional support and acceptance by her classmates more than support in learning English. TC's use of Russian was intentional because the other students in her class (all Spanish speakers) had initially been hesitant to interact with Tanya because of her different language background. TC's approach to getting to know her students played an important part in bringing Tanya into the community of her classroom and in building trust between her and Tanya. TC's practice was humanizing because she created ways for Tanya and her Spanish-speaking students to connect with each other, breaking down the linguistic barriers that students perceived. She made all students' home languages welcome in her classroom, creating mutual respect between students, and between her and her students. In doing so, she created an environment in which students felt they could be themselves and open up to her and to one another.

TAKE ACTION IN YOUR CLASSROOM

- Find out about your students' home languages and English language backgrounds by asking them, their families, previous teachers, intake office, school counselors, and by reading their files.
- Find out about your students' literacy in English and in their home languages by consulting previous test scores, using informal assessments, asking a colleague who speaks their home language to read a text with the student in their home language, and/or asking the student to write down their name, where they are from, and one interest in either their home language or English, depending on what they are able to do.
- To find out more about your students' prior schooling, read your students' intake files, ask your school counselor, read school files from prior education, and ask prior teachers. Ask students and their families about the frequency and duration of prior school attendance, content covered, and format and delivery of lessons.
- To find out about students' interests, ask them! Depending upon students' English language proficiency levels, and your capability in students' home languages, this could be answered by their circling pictures of activities they like, raising their hand when an image is shown that represents something that they like, making a collage or drawing a picture that represent their interests, or responding verbally or in writing to questions about their interests. You can also eat lunch with students, spend time on the playground, offer homework help before or after school or during lunch, and help with school clubs and extracurriculars that provide opportunities to spend time with students outside class. Daily check-ins with students are also helpful.
- To find out about students' experiences at home and in their community, look at intake paperwork and ask your school counselor. You can also ask your students to tell you about them. This can be done in the form of stories or drawings. You can also find out about their families, home lives, and where and with whom they live through phone conversations with their families (with an interpreter if needed), home surveys (keeping in mind the home language and literacy when using these), conferences with parents/caregivers, and home visits.

- If you do not live in the same area as your students, get to know your students' communities through conversations with heads of community resources in their areas (for example, community centers, clubs, libraries, and churches), volunteering in the community, participating in community events and activities, and shopping in the community.

QUESTIONS FOR REFLECTION

1. Can you think of a time when a teacher really made an effort to get to know you? What did that teacher do? How did that make you feel, and what impact did it have on your learning? How do the efforts by your teacher relate to ways of knowing multilingual students shared here?
2. What ideas do you get from this chapter about what you would like to use to get to know your multilingual students? Are there some techniques you already use? Can you give a specific example?
3. What are some challenges to getting to know multilingual students? How can you address or overcome these?

NOTES

1. We use the term *minoritized*, rather than *minority*, to recognize that even when multilingual students represent a majority in a school, due to inequitable relations of power that are supported through particular policies and practices they are often positioned as nondominant because of their language, culture, income, religion, and other factors (Flores & Rosa, 2015; Peercy et al., 2019b).

2. In pull-out lessons, teachers pull students out of their grade-level classroom for individual or small-group instruction to support their language development and make classroom content more accessible. In plug-in lessons, another teacher joins the grade-level teacher in the classroom, sometimes working with small groups of students, and sometimes coteaching the class in a variety of formats. Plug-in instruction is also referred to as push-in instruction in some contexts, because the teacher "pushes in" to the grade-level classroom rather than pulling students out of the classroom.

CHAPTER 2

Building a Positive Learning Environment

> Not having high classroom management standards and behavioral and procedural expectations for the kids is a really big problem for ESOL students because if their classroom is chaotic, it is hard even for me to think in the room, let alone for somebody who's trying to learn a new language. Having good procedures is particularly important for ESOL students, because they need an extra barrier from stress and extra structure.
>
> —Chris, secondary ESOL teacher

A positive learning environment is an important aspect of humanizing pedagogy for any learner. All students need both structure and support to thrive. However, as Chris's thoughts above illustrate, creating such conditions for learning are especially important for multilingual students. Learning a new language and new content at the same time, possibly while also having to adjust to a new culture, is in itself both cognitively and emotionally taxing. As we will discuss in this chapter, multilingual students are also subject to several other factors that create a need for an especially supportive classroom environment.

Creating a positive learning environment is a complex task. It means planning, selecting, managing, and organizing not only physical classroom objects and instructional materials, but also learning activities, grouping structures, and learning sequences in a manner that contributes to the students' learning. In this process, you need to consider not only students' academic and language needs, but also their social-emotional needs.

DIMENSIONS OF BUILDING A POSITIVE LEARNING ENVIRONMENT

In this chapter we will discuss building a positive classroom environment for multilingual students through:

- Clear procedures, consistent routines, and high expectations
- The use of culturally and linguistically responsive and sustaining pedagogy
- Development of students' social-emotional skills

To engage in this core practice means that you need to carefully consider how language, culture, and prior experiences impact multilingual students, and how you can rethink and reorganize your classroom spaces, routines, and expectations to ensure students are academically successful and physically and emotionally safe (Caldera et al., 2020; Haneda, 2014; Siwatu et al., 2017). It also means questioning the hidden assumptions you have about how students should act and interact, and considering how you could make your classroom more congruent with the students' linguistic and cultural backgrounds (Delpit, 1988; Milner & Tenore, 2010; Paris & Alim, 2017). Finally, creating a positive classroom environment also means supporting students in developing important social-emotional skills and making sure you are providing affirming, healing interactions within your classroom community, especially among students who are suffering from trauma (Castro-Olivo, 2014; Castro-Olivo et al., 2011). We examine each of these ways of building a positive learning environment in the sections that follow.

Clear Procedures, Consistent Routines, and High Expectations

Multilingual students often experience a school day that is more fragmented than that of other students. For example, they may receive small-group instruction from several teachers in different settings throughout the day. Andrew, an elementary ESOL teacher, described the difficulties this poses for students: "Expectations are different in different groups, or sometimes it's hard for students to be like, 'Okay, when I'm in a small group, it feels like this and looks like this, and when I'm in a large group, it feels like this and looks like this.'"

In addition, multilingual students may "feel anxious and unsure in classrooms where there is little consistency in how things are approached and inadequate instructions for how to proceed with activities" (Olsen, 2012, p. 18). Given the wide variety in their schedules and settings, as well as different prior cultural and schooling experiences, which impact multilingual students in particular, it is no wonder many of them feel like they are not in control of their own educational paths (Dabach, 2014). Clear procedures, consistent routines, and high expectations that support multilingual students' learning are therefore an important way to ensure that they can fully and equitably participate in your classroom activities.

Feeling lost in the myriad of classroom routines that other students seem to know instinctively may be especially pronounced for two categories of multilingual students. One of these groups is newcomers who may be new to your school, state, or even to the country. Another group is often called SLIFE

(DeCapua & Marshall, 2011), or students who have had limited exposure to formal schooling in any country. Refugee background students often fall into this category. For these students, it can be difficult to learn the "complex, and often hidden" procedures, routines, and rules "that constitute the expected learning paradigm of Western-style education" (DeCapua & Marshall, 2011, p. 3). Consider, for example, the number of routines students are expected to know when first entering a classroom:

> Where do I put my things? Where can I sit? What materials should I take out? What activity do I begin? Do I need to turn anything in? Am I allowed to talk? How should I address the teacher?

Consequently, teachers may need to teach students procedures for even "seemingly mundane behaviors like raising one's hand to ask a question, asking permission to use the bathroom, or speaking and writing in complete sentences" (Caldera et al., 2020, p. 354). However, this does not mean simply expecting students to assimilate to the school's norms, nor does it mean that you should uncritically enforce classroom or school rules without questioning their impact on students. In fact, you can and should involve students in jointly negotiating classroom procedures, routines, and norms (Newbould, 2018; Rafferty, 2007). For example, you can use a whole-class meeting to create a social contract that outlines the rights and responsibilities of both students and you for the entire school year, as well as conduct smaller check-ins to agree on the steps and procedures for any new type of a classroom activity. This way you can ensure procedures build up to routines that support student learning.

When designing classroom procedures and routines, it is important to pair them with high expectations for student learning and conduct—to anticipate that all students will excel in your class by using the procedures and routines you have taught them. In other words, teachers should *expect* students to display "a posture, consciousness, and disposition of learning and engagement in the classroom" (Milner & Tenore, 2010, p. 594), while simultaneously *showing* them how they are developed. Insisting that students succeed in your classroom is an important part of humanizing the education of multilingual students, because without this insistence, classroom norms and procedures will be nothing more than a system of control over students. An important part of holding high expectations is advocating that students be treated in the same manner in all their classrooms. Chapter 6 will discuss this type of advocacy in more detail.

Teachers who combine high expectations with genuine care and concern over their minoritized students' futures and successes have sometimes been called "warm demanders" (Ross et al., 2008). Chris expressed: "I like 'warm demander.' I try to regulate my emotional response to student behavior by keeping that phrase in mind. Stay warm, don't destroy the relationship with a highly negative reaction, yet continue to demand a focus on learning and effort."

Being a warm demander can also be described with the Spanish word *cariño*, or "authentic care and respect" (Bartolomé, 2008, p. 1). Both concepts involve not only expecting that students succeed, but also exposing and dismantling structures that hold them back. As Bartolomé (2008) puts it, teachers who practice *cariño* understand that "caring for and loving one's subordinated students is insufficient unless the love and care are informed by authentic respect and a desire to equalize unequal learning conditions in school" (p. 2). One way you can begin equalizing students' learning conditions is to enact culturally and linguistically responsive and sustaining pedagogy, described in the next section.

Culturally and Linguistically Responsive and Sustaining Pedagogy

While consistent routines are helpful, it is important not to rely on them to such an extent that it erases your responsiveness to each student's individual needs and your school context as a whole. Instead, as Milner and colleagues (2018) note, "Classroom management practices must be equitable and attentive to the particulars of the context . . . practices cannot be developed and enacted synonymously across contexts but should be based on the situational realities of the learning environment" (p. 12). This responsiveness to students' realities has been variously called culturally responsive pedagogy, culturally relevant pedagogy, culturally sustaining pedagogy, or specifically with linguistic differences in mind, culturally and linguistically responsive pedagogy (Gay, 2006; Ladson-Billings, 1995; Lucas, Villegas, & Freedson-Gonzalez, 2008; Paris & Alim, 2017). We have chosen to use the term *culturally and linguistically responsive/sustaining pedagogy* (CLRP) to encompass these approaches, which all aim to create a classroom environment that is tailored to students' needs. CLRP consists of a few basic principles, including:

- Valuing students' cultural and linguistic backgrounds as an essential part of their identity
- Building on students' existing cultural and linguistic practices and knowledge to help them learn
- Advocating for the maintenance and development of students' multiculturalism and multilingualism

By taking these considerations into account, you can make sure that the resulting learning environment is "conducive to high levels of learning . . . personally comfortable, racially and ethnically inclusive, and intellectually stimulating" (Gay, 2006, p. 343).

One way you can make your classroom more linguistically responsive is by allowing students to use all of their languages and language varieties for both learning and socializing. Often called translanguaging, this approach is based on the idea that it is natural for people who are multilingual to continuously and flexibly switch between languages (García & Lin, 2017). As we discussed in Chapter 1, translanguaging is possible even if you don't speak your students' home languages, and simply attempting to use some of your students' language is important, as TC, a secondary ESOL science teacher, explained:

> With my French-speaking students, we have fun, because I cannot pronounce any words in French, but I let them know, "It's okay, I'm learning it just like you're learning English. And it's okay if I have an accent in your language, because it's not my first language. But at least I'm trying." When they see that I'm respecting where they come from, that I'm respecting their language and it may not be perfect, but at least I'm trying, they kind of get the same attitude of, "As long as I try, it will be okay." And it's okay to have fun with learning, and laugh at yourself or just appreciate the fact that you're here and be proud of yourself for being here.

Some things you can do to create a positive learning environment by translanguaging in your classroom:

- Learn to greet students in their home languages as they come into the classroom.
- Give directions both orally and in writing, using multiple languages. Have students interpret directions for one another in their home languages.
- Provide multilingual instructional materials and allow students to access multilingual sources available online.
- Use humor, such as puns, and play with language to build rapport with students.

For example, Andrew described how a translanguaging routine using greetings in his 2nd-grade students' home languages got started:

> I recently put up lots of different flags from countries my students come from. Under each one it says "hello and welcome" in students' corresponding home languages. I noticed almost immediately the kids came in and they were like, "El Salvador, Ethiopia, the Philippines!" Everyone was really excited about it and then each one said "hello" and "welcome" in their language to each other. Now it's how I'll start a lesson and I think it's helped them feel like, "Oh, my flag is here too." Especially if a student's from, say, the Philippines, I only have two students from there who speak Tagalog at home, and I see they enjoy getting a chance to show off and share a little bit of their culture with the rest of the group.

As Andrew noted, translanguaging that involved just two phrases in each student's language had a big impact on the learning environment, making students feel like their countries and languages were represented. TC also uses translanguaging for building rapport with her students. For example, during one lesson she had a friendly exchange when she explained to her students that she would be absent the next day. TC playfully asked her students, "¿Van a extrañarme?" [Are you going to miss me?], to which some students said "Sí" [yes] while others said "No." TC then jokingly warned the latter group, "Minus point!" making everyone laugh. Chris noted that such exchanges can create a positive learning environment for the students and teacher alike, saying, "I learned that I could be silly and be myself in front of the students. This has made all of the difference in the world. It makes me love my job, and it helps the students feel like my classroom is a place they want to be."

Another way to build a culturally and linguistically responsive classroom is to understand the ways students prefer to learn or are accustomed to learning. For example, some students may come from schooling traditions that emphasize memorization and repetition, while others may be used to working collectively and collaboratively rather than completing individual assignments. Yet other students might be used to copying text straight from sources because they have learned that they should rely on what experts have said about the topic. Understanding that these habits are cultural rather than the students "being difficult" is an important part of building a culturally responsive learning environment because you can help students understand how expectations in your classroom and school are similar and/or different from what they are accustomed to.

To find out more about your students' preferred and familiar ways of learning, you can use methods for getting to know students outlined in Chapter 1. Knowing how your students like to learn will help you select activities and materials that will feel familiar to them, as will be further described in Chapter 3. For example, when teachers choose instructional resources that are meaningful to students because of their cultural heritage, they not only show recognition of students' cultures but also provide a bridge between the students' experiences and what is required of them at school (Orosco & O'Connor, 2014).

It is also important to recognize that there is no single "best" way to learn, and that you can build on students' existing practices while also showing them how to learn in new ways. Haneda (2014) suggests building this type of classroom environment by creating meaningful lesson activities around students' lived experiences and interests; helping students participate in school practices through collaborating with others; encouraging students to use all of their linguistic and literacy skills for meaning-making—including those they've learned outside school; and supporting students to acquire the skills involved in collaborative school activities.

For example, as students work on a research project, you can point out and praise their existing strengths in managing and completing tasks, such as their ability to work together, recognize important sources, organize their materials efficiently, help their peers understand information, use several languages to access information, or copy information accurately. TC frequently reminded her students of their language abilities, such as when she told students, "You already know these words in English *and . . .*" and her students finished her sentence by saying "Spanish," which TC followed up with, "Okay? Because we bilingual." You can also show students how to build on their existing abilities. For example, you can teach students to take on responsibility for an individual task within a group research project, express their ideas from sources in their own words while giving credit to the original source, use a new type of organizer or system to keep their notes, or use a rubric to help peer- or self-evaluate their work.

Melissa, a secondary ESOL ELA teacher, described how she tailored her lesson on question types according to students' English proficiency levels, while also providing an opportunity for them to build on their skills by learning from their peers. Her beginning-level students were tasked with investigating and composing yes/no questions, while intermediate-level students worked on WH-questions, and advanced level students worked on questions with modal verbs, such as "Can you help me?" and "Should I pick her up?" In addition, students worked together in collaborative groups that provided scaffolding through the opening and closing discussions in the lesson, which helped all students in the group learn each other's question types.

Finally, you can teach students that there are a variety of ways they can engage with content. For example, you can demonstrate how an activity would look while working alone versus with a partner; teach how to pick a leveled text from among several of varying difficulty; have students read across genres (e.g., a scientific article, an autobiography of a scientist, and a sci-fi graphic novel) and point out the ways each can inform them; show models of a variety of finished products students can choose from to demonstrate their learning (such as a video or an essay); and so on. The last point is connected to an important practice we will be discussing in more depth in Chapter 3: differentiation. Your practice for creating and managing a positive classroom environment should be differentiated to support your particular students and context just as you should differentiate your instructional practice.

Development of Students' Social-Emotional Skills

While considering multilingual students' academic and language needs is important for their success, we also cannot overlook students as social and emotional individuals (Carter Andrews & Castillo, 2016). All humans have a need to connect with others socially and emotionally. Supportive and trusting relationships between teachers and students are key factors in learning. However, for multilingual students, especially those in the beginning stages of developing English, it may be difficult to form such relationships with you or to develop friendships and participate in the social life of a school through extracurricular activities (Castro-Olivo et al., 2011). There is evidence that when multilingual students' instructional programs only focus on language and ignore the development of their social-emotional skills, students end up with lower levels of resiliency, or the ability to cope with setbacks, as well as acculturation, or the healthy adaptation to their new cultural context (Castro-Olivo et al., 2011).

Many schools today understand the need for social-emotional learning (SEL) for all students' mental health, and teachers are being trained in programs that provide direct instruction in SEL skills such as self-regulation, conflict resolution, and relationship-building (CASEL, 2021). However, it is important to consider how these programs may need to be adapted for multilingual students' needs. For example, family members can be powerful partners in an SEL program, but multilingual families may find it difficult to get involved in their students' schooling for a host of reasons, including childcare and work demands, lack of English proficiency, and a cultural unfamiliarity with U.S. schools' expectations for family engagement. However, schools can offer outreach programs to overcome these barriers (Niehaus & Adelson, 2014). Chapter 6 discusses working with families in further detail.

SEL programs may also need to be adapted to match students' cultural expectations. For example, Castro-Olivo (2014) modified a SEL program called *Strong Teens* for Latino students by translating the materials into Spanish (*Jóvenes Fuertes*), and adding lessons on relevant topics such as acculturation stress, as well as having the whole program evaluated by a focus group consisting of people from the students' cultural background. With any SEL approach, it is important to consider whether the program is culturally adapted for your students, and whether there is a need for any modifications.

In addition to the need to help students develop their social-emotional skills, there is growing recognition that teachers need to be aware of possible trauma, especially among their multilingual students (Crosby et al., 2018; Hood, 2018). This is because multilingual students are often part of minoritized racial and socioeconomic groups, which can expose them to trauma-inducing experiences (Tienda & Haskins, 2011), such as:

- Racism and language-based discrimination
- Violence in their homes and communities
- Crime and incarceration
- Inadequate housing and nutrition
- Lack of mental and physical health care

In addition, refugee and immigrant students may have fled war, hunger, or gang violence in their home countries, experienced mistreatment during the immigration process, and may continue to fear for their safety and/or the safety of their family members even after arriving in the United States (McIntyre et al., 2011). The teachers we worked with were keenly aware of these possible sources of trauma for their students, and Chris shared the importance of such awareness: "The very first thing you need to do is make kids feel comfortable, especially beginner ESOL students. Students who are coming with a lot of trauma and really difficult circumstances in their home lives are not going to come to school unless they feel comfortable."

Trauma-informed teaching is a complex approach that we can't fully delve into in this book, although at the end of this book we provide additional resources for learning more about this topic. One of the most important things to know about trauma is that adverse experiences can literally change the developing brain and cause students to go into a fight-or-flight mode, even in situations that you, as a teacher, might not consider could trigger such a response.

One way for you to think about responding to students who may be experiencing trauma is to integrate a multi-tiered system of support (MTSS), an approach that aims to proactively support students at different levels of need (see Figure 2.1).

At the lowest tier of support, you should consistently use affective, caring language to praise and reaffirm *all* students. For example, Erica begins her lessons by asking each of her elementary school students how they are feeling that day. This provides both a brief check-in point for her and an opportunity for students to feel cared for by their teacher. In addition, she explained how she modulates even her tone and volume when speaking to students she knows have experienced trauma: "This one student is hesitant around certain things that a lot of his peers aren't, so I'm not as strict and firm. I'm a lot quieter. I change little things, like my voice. Thinking about their background influences not only instruction, but also discipline, demeanor, the volume of your voice, just everything."

Figure 2.1. Examples of multitiered supports for behavior and social-emotional learning

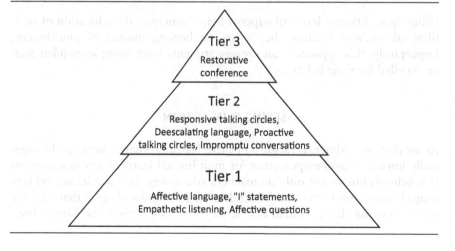

Tier 3
Restorative
conference

Tier 2
Responsive talking circles,
Deescalating language, Proactive
talking circles, Impromptu conversations

Tier 1
Affective language, "I" statements,
Empathetic listening, Affective questions

Middle-level tiers of support involve using regular, proactive talking circles to discuss things that matter to students in order to help them build relationships with one another and prevent conflicts before they emerge (Mirsky, 2011). In these circles, students and the teacher meet to discuss classroom events such as upcoming assessments, field trips, athletic schedules; happenings around the community and in the students' homes; as well as news topics that students want to bring up. When conflicts do arise, you can use smaller impromptu conversations and de-escalating language to help students step back from the emotional upheaval of the moment. For example, you can ask students to take a break, do breathing exercises, or describe what they feel in their body and mind before reflecting on what they might do in the future if negative feelings start building up. You can also conduct small-group or whole-class responsive circles to discuss the conflict, let students reflect on each other's words, and think of solutions together to restore peace (Mirsky, 2011).

At the highest tier, restorative justice circles can bring offenders and those affected together to discuss what has happened and what needs to be done to repair the harm done (Mansfield et al., 2018). At this tier, you might seek help from other staff who are experienced in restorative justice, such as your school counselor, or even people from outside the school such as religious leaders or youth advocates. Nancy, a secondary ESOL teacher described her need to learn how to run these circles:

> One thing I want to start doing is either doing community building or a restorative justice session for whatever has happened that week. For example, if students didn't do work when a substitute was here, or there was a fight between two students, or something happened where a student was just not listening to me that week, I want to make it a regular routine where I feel comfortable facilitating a restorative justice circle myself.

Using these different levels of support helps humanize the education of multilingual students because they focus on healing instead of punishment. Importantly, this approach can prevent students from being suspended and/ or expelled for their behavior.

SEEING IT IN ACTION

As we discussed above, creating a positive learning environment can be especially important and empowering for multilingual learners whose success in U.S. schools hinges not only on teachers addressing their academic and language learning needs, but also the kinds of social-emotional needs that their life experiences may have created. Below, we show how Andrea and Chris—both

ESOL teachers—humanize the management of their classrooms through clear procedures and consistent routines, culturally and linguistically responsive pedagogy, and the development of their students' social-emotional skills.

Andrea

During Andrea's internship in an elementary school, she frequently worked with a group of five 3rd-graders by plugging into their classroom and conducting her lessons around a small table. Andrea's students were mostly Spanish-speaking—a fact that, combined with her own Spanish proficiency, made it more feasible for her to leverage her students' home languages in her classroom. In the vignette, notice how Andrea guides students through the lesson by using consistent routines combined with culturally and linguistically responsive pedagogical moves such as translanguaging and letting students choose a writing topic directly related to their own lives.

Andrea begins by walking students through the lesson objective, which reads, "I can brainstorm events in my morning and select one moment to write about." Throughout the conversation about the objective, she translanguages in Spanish, eliciting the words *momento* [moment], *evento* [event] and *mañana* [morning] from the students, who are visibly eager to share their knowledge of their home language. One student triumphantly raises his hands in the air when he comes up with the word *evento*. Then, Andrea tells students she will show them some examples, opens a picture dictionary, and displays it on the table for the students. She points at pictures of different rooms as she recounts events from her morning.

Andrea: Let me think . . . I saw my daughter because she woke up. And what else did I do? This is another page. I was in my kitchen. (She points to the picture of a kitchen.) I was packing lunch for my daughter. I was eating breakfast. (She mimes eating.) I went to the bathroom. I brushed my teeth. (She mimes brushing her teeth.) Our story is going to be about *my* morning. (She writes "my morning" on a flip chart.) But Yesenia, you're not going to write about my morning. You're going to write about *Yesenia's* morning. And Henry, you're going to write about *Henry's* morning.

Andrea gestures to each student and repeats this direction to illustrate how each student will write about their own morning. Then, she models writing key phrases with the help of the picture dictionary.

Andrea: Let's see, I brushed my teeth this morning. I'm going to look in the picture dictionary for the words.

Andrea points to the picture of brushing teeth and turns to write on a piece of paper displayed on an easel, "brushed my teeth." She says this out loud as she writes.

Andrea: What else did I do this morning?
Francisco: Eat breakfast!
Andrea: I ate my breakfast! (She mimes eating, then turns to write "eat my breakfast.") What else did I do? I drove to school. (Mimes driving.) I know you probably walked, Edgar. Or did you drive a car to school this morning?
Students laugh.
Andrea: Did you drive to school? (Writes "drive to school.")
Edgar: My mom.
Andrea: What else did I do this morning? I woke up! I forgot about that! I woke up.

Andrea writes this on the piece of paper, then she takes the piece of paper off the easel and puts it in the center of the table.

Andrea: Now that I have my ideas, I'm going to choose just one. Which one would make a good story?

Students lean forward and point to phrases on the paper to indicate what they think would make a good story. The group picks "waking up" and Andrea tells them she will sketch the steps of the event. She models drawing quick stick-figure sketches and models retelling the event with the words first, next, then, and last. Lastly, she instructs students to begin brainstorming their list with the help of a partner and a picture dictionary. Students begin working, with Andrea providing additional support as needed.

As the lesson example illustrates, Andrea explained and modeled the writing activity in a detailed manner while using translanguaging and gesturing to make her instructions comprehensible (for more on comprehensible input, see Chapter 3). In addition to her proficiency in Spanish, Andrea knew some American Sign Language, which she drew on to come up with consistent gestures for words, thereby ensuring students understood her classroom routines. She explained: "I try to find signs or riff off of the signs, so that the hand signal itself, or the body language itself incorporates the meaning of the word into it, to make sure that the student is not only getting a whole-body experience of figuring out what this word means but is also associating the meaning with speaking the word out loud."

In the above lesson, students were at different levels of English proficiency. However, Andrea used several different strategies to ensure students had clear procedures and consistent routines that would support their learning.

By starting the lesson with objectives, using an I-do, we-do, you-do approach to the lesson, and selecting an easily approachable topic, she helped even her beginning-level students take part in the lesson. In addition, connecting brainstorming and drafting skills and the concept of sequenced events to students' own experiences of morning routines built on students' existing knowledge while introducing new words and phrases in English. This, combined with Andrea's intentional use of students' home languages as a resource, demonstrated her responsiveness to students' cultural and linguistic assets. The resulting lesson was inclusive and responsive to students' strengths and needs, yet directed toward the development of important skills—a good example of humanizing pedagogy.

Chris

During his internship, Chris, an experienced paraeducator who had previously worked with multilingual learners in middle school, taught 9th grade to mostly Spanish-speaking students with beginning-level proficiency in English. His student body was highly transient—five of his students had enrolled in the class in the last week. His lesson is focused on describing the setting and making predictions about a book called *The Most Beautiful Place in the World*. In the lesson excerpt and the following comments from Chris, notice how he taps into students' interests in a culturally and linguistically responsive manner with his translanguaging and his choice of a book about a young boy in Guatemala, and implements clear procedures and consistent routines so that even his newcomers can participate in the lesson and meet high expectations. Finally, notice how Chris recognizes the students' social-emotional needs by giving them a break.

> Chris passes out the book and displays a Powerpoint slide that has the word "setting" and its Spanish translation, *escenario*. He explains that the setting of *The Most Beautiful Place in the World* is San Pablo La Laguna, Guatemala. He displays the cover of the book on the screen.
>
> *Chris:* What do we see on the cover?
> *Students:* (Call out answers.) Boy. Mountain. Water.
> *Chris:* What type of water is that?
> *Estela:* Lake.
>
> Chris turns to the first page and begins to read aloud, stopping frequently to clarify words by providing the Spanish translation or acting out the word.
>
> *Chris:* I am going to read. When I stop reading, say the next word. "My name is Juan. I live in Guatemala, in the mountains. My town, San

Pablo, has three huge volcanoes near it, and high cliffs all around it, and steep, bright green fields of corn and garlic and onions growing in the hills, and red coffee berries growing in the shade of big trees in the valleys."

Chris stops about once every sentence to clarify words with gestures and in Spanish. Students are engaged and murmuring additional Spanish translations to each other.

Chris: (Reads to the students.) "It has lots of flowers and birds—eagles and orioles and owls, hummingbirds, and flocks of wild—" (He stops to wait for students to read the next word.)
Students: Parrots.
Chris: ¿Cómo se dice en español "parrots"? Pájaros que pueden hablar. [How do you say "parrots" in Spanish? Birds that can speak.]

Students aren't sure of the word. Finally, one student says *loro* [parrot].

Later during the lesson, Chris helped students create predictions about the rest of the story. In our debrief conversation, he noted:

I think that all the kids were able to understand the content of the story through talking about it, translating certain words. The prediction exercise I think went well. Even the ones who weren't able to produce a prediction in English understood the context (of the story) and had a relevant idea even if they could only communicate it in Spanish.

The way Chris attended to his students' needs, given that many of them were beginners or had just arrived in the country, ensured that they were able to meet the expectation of making predictions from the story. Bridging the linguistic gap for the students rather than giving these students an easier task showed Chris's ability to position his students as capable learners and knowers.

At the end of the same lesson, Chris told his students to stay in their seats until the bell rang, though they could take out their phones. During our debrief, Chris explained: "I give them two breaks every class where they're allowed to take out their cell phones and text or listen to music or whatever. And the tradeoff is they can't have it out at all when it's not a break."

Chris used his knowledge of students' social-emotional needs as he allowed students to take a break and use their phones. The two-break routine gave students a respite from the cognitively taxing task of using English and cut down on unauthorized use of cell phones when it was time for students to concentrate. With this routine, Chris also helped students learn a valuable skill of alternating focused learning time and taking breaks to do something enjoyable. His teaching was humanizing because it brought students' resources to the classroom and recognized students' social-emotional needs in addition to their academic needs.

TAKE ACTION IN YOUR CLASSROOM

- To create clear and consistent procedures, try writing out the steps to a learning activity you are planning to include in your lesson in as much detail as you can. Writing out each step can help you realize how complex an activity may be for students who aren't familiar with the activity culturally or linguistically. Think about what your students might already know about performing the activity. Then, think about which of the steps you will need to teach students so that they can be successful with the activity. Lastly, use the same steps consistently so that the procedure becomes a routine that students can feel comfortable following.

- Maintain high expectations for your students by continuously monitoring students' performance and offering them a higher-level text, activity, or group as soon as they seem ready. Give students additional support as needed so that they can feel successful with reaching the new, higher expectations.

- Choose and implement procedures that support student learning. For example, if you know students will need to produce several short essays throughout the year, make sure to design a procedure that will break the essay writing into parts and then approach each part the same way each time. For example, consistently use the same kind of outlining organizer so that students can feel comfortable using the same procedure even when the topic changes.

- To implement culturally and linguistically responsive and sustaining pedagogy, think about what resources you can leverage. Do you speak other languages? What do you know about your students' cultures? How can you let your students be the teachers and learn from them? What resources does your school or district have, such as bilingual family liaisons? How can you learn more from students' families? Then, partner with people who can provide support. Learn to look critically at your lesson materials and activities through a culturally and linguistically sensitive lens.

- Develop students' social-emotional skills as part of your everyday instruction. For example, ask students to reflect on how they felt during the lesson and provide them the vocabulary to express their feelings in a nuanced way (e.g., by teaching them words like *frustrated*, *disappointed*, or *hopeful*). Develop and use protocols for structured collaboration among students. Use affective language such

as "I feel proud when you . . ." and "We'll get through it together,"
and encourage students to show care toward one another.

QUESTIONS FOR REFLECTION

1. What procedures do you need to teach students in your classroom?
2. What resources and skills do you already have to create a linguistically
   and culturally responsive and sustaining classroom? How can you
   learn more about your students' languages and cultures?
3. How prepared are you to address social-emotional learning in your
   classroom? How can you learn more about your students' social-
   emotional needs?

CHAPTER 3

Content and Language Instruction

I always start with a goal of what my students need to accomplish or master, and work from there. That process also involves matching goals with content standards and language standards. For me, the challenging part is that a lesson or unit has many possibilities and can go in many different directions. Identifying the goals and standards does not give teachers a clear, linear path to an effective lesson plan. Teachers still have to plan how to present new information, how they will engage students in meaningful ways, and how to support students' understanding.

—Andrew, elementary ESOL teacher

As Andrew notes, planning effective instruction involves attending to content and language standards, deciding how to present information in ways that engage students, and determining what will best support student comprehension. Furthermore, the teachers in our group often commented that knowing their students well led to more effective planning and instruction. Thus, you will notice many connections between how well you know your students and your ability to plan and enact instruction that is effective and responsive, and that positions students as competent and knowledgeable contributors to your classroom. Most important to remember is that your goal is to provide high-quality, appropriately challenging instruction that helps multilingual students engage with the same kinds of content and materials as their English-dominant peers to achieve their highest potential.

DIMENSIONS OF PLANNING AND ENACTING INSTRUCTION

We found that the teachers' use of the following dimensions of this core practice allowed them to plan and enact instruction that met students at their current language and content levels while also introducing challenging and meaningful new content and language:

- Comprehensible input
- Scaffolding

- Differentiation
- Integrated content and language objectives

Research shows that when language learners receive input that is reduced in complexity (through techniques such as repetition, paraphrasing, slower speech rate, and simplification of complex utterances), they have greater potential to understand and acquire new language (Long, 1983; Saito & Akiyama, 2018), and keep up with peers (Aguirre-Muñoz & Boscardin, 2008); therefore, providing comprehensible input is an important part of supporting language learning. Scaffolding is also critical because it provides the right amount of support (neither too little nor too much) for students to be challenged while also accessing the meaning of new content and/or new language (Gibbons, 2003, 2015; Maybin et al., 1992). Differentiation—or the modification of content, learning processes, or the end product that students create (Tomlinson, 2008, 2014)—is also fundamental for teaching multilingual students because it allows students to learn new information in a variety of ways, depending on their pre-existing strengths and needs (Brown & Endo, 2017). Finally, integrated content and language instruction is pivotal for language development (Baecher et al., 2014; Lyster, 2007), and clear objectives for that integrated instruction are important for supporting high-quality learning (Goldenberg, 2013).

Comprehensible Input

Lee and VanPatten (2003) point out how important it is that teachers know that all students, even students with beginning levels of language proficiency, can begin to understand a new language. As they note, "The belief that beginning language learners cannot understand anything is simply that—a belief. Imagine what life would be like if parents believed the same thing about their one-year-olds: No one would ever acquire a language!" (p. 33). Of course, one-year-olds do learn language, partially because of the ways many parents and caregivers modify their speech when speaking to their children—for example, by repeating words or pointing at objects while talking about them. For students learning additional languages, especially in the school context, it is even more important that the language they hear and see is intentionally modified to be more understandable and accessible to them. Krashen (1985) termed this modified language as "comprehensible input."

Krashen stated that language is acquired by receiving comprehensible input slightly above one's current level of competence (input + 1, or i + 1). Thus, challenging, yet accessible, input is important for multilingual students' acquisition of English. Though Krashen's construct of comprehensible input has been critiqued for being ambiguous (e.g., Liu, 2015), the concept of modifying the kind of language input your students receive so that it is more understandable is a powerful one. Think about how differently you would comprehend simple instructions in a language you do not know to, say, write your name at the top of a page if it were modeled for you through actions and examples, rather than your simply being told, "write your name at the top of the page."

Comprehensible input involves providing many different types of extralinguistic support. By extralinguistic support, we mean approaches that are outside of spoken language, such as using gestures, acting out, displaying images, and showing students real items (often called realia) that are being discussed (for example, maps, travel tickets, food, classroom objects, clothing, and so on). Teachers can also make their input comprehensible in several other ways (Hatch, 1983), including:

- Slowing the rate of their speech and including more pauses
- Placing stress on important nouns
- Enunciating clearly
- Using more high-frequency words and defining key words
- Using short sentences, repetition, and rephrasing
- Offering possible answers after asking a question

In the lessons that we observed, we saw many examples of teachers using comprehensible input to support multilingual students:

- Andrew demonstrated the concept of beginning, middle, and end of the story the class had read by pointing several times to his shoulder to indicate beginning, his elbow for middle, and his wrist for end.
- Erica encouraged William, an elementary newcomer student, to push his chair under his desk when he got up by having another student model what to do after she said, "Push your chair in," and then giving the same prompt to William who was then able to understand what it meant.
- Kendall showed her elementary students how to start a new entry in their journals by modeling with an example journal.
- Chris acted out basic verbs like "run," "jump," and "eat" so that a secondary ESOL ELA student could preview activities in the book she would be listening to.
- TC showed a close-captioned video about photosynthesis to her secondary ESOL science students to introduce the process and main vocabulary related to it.
- Melissa taught *Romeo and Juliet* by having her secondary ESOL ELA students read and watch a modern version of the play alongside the Shakespearean version.

Students' access to content makes a tremendous difference in their ability to participate in school and feel that they are valued members of the classroom.

Comprehensible input is therefore a key aspect of creating a humanizing experience for your multilingual students.

Scaffolding

Scaffolding has its origins in Vygotskian sociocultural theory, which says that learners can do something on their own after first being given appropriate support to build their understanding (Vygotsky, 1962, 1978). We define scaffolding as both preplanned and in-the-moment temporary support provided by a more capable or knowledgeable person. The person providing scaffolding is often the teacher, but it can also include peers.

Scaffolding is an important means for addressing academic and linguistic differences between English-dominant students and multilingual students, which can decrease inequity within the educational system (Reyes, 2017; Salazar, 2013). Thus, when teachers are able to scaffold effectively, they humanize their teaching by helping their multilingual students to meaningfully participate in instruction (Ramirez et al., 2017).

Scaffolding helps a learner more readily accomplish a task and move toward greater independence. Scaffolding might look like the following activities:

- Providing guided notes in the form of an organizer with some parts, such as key words, already filled in
- Previewing and interacting with key vocabulary before engaging with content that uses the new vocabulary
- Providing sentence starters, sentence frames, or a word bank
- Demonstrating a set of procedures or directions
- Sharing models or examples of what a final product looks like
- Using check-in points or steps to build toward a final product
- Having students discuss ideas with peers and/or teacher
- Using an outline or visual structure to identify key points

Scaffolding can also be a planned progression throughout an activity, a lesson, a unit, or even the quarter or whole school year, in which you create support toward a new concept, gradually moving students toward greater independence. The following are examples of scaffolding as a progression:

- Moving from teacher demonstration and modeling to students working in small groups or pairs, in order to independently create something related to the new learning
- Introducing collaborative work by first setting expectations for what successful group work looks like, then establishing group roles and rules, and finally introducing the collaborative task, as we see in one of Melissa's lessons (see Chapter 7)

When you are preparing lessons, think about what you want students to be able to do by the end of a lesson or unit, and consider where they are right now and what resources they bring to the lesson. Then think about how you can draw on their existing resources and the kinds of support you can create that will help them to get to that end point. Scaffolding includes both this kind of advanced planning as well as noticing in the midst of lessons where you might need to include additional support that helps your learners.

For instance, in a lesson on opinions, Kendall noticed that her 3rd-grade students were hesitant to respond to the question, "What is an opinion?" She had planned for students to share their response to the question with partners as a way to launch the lesson. However, noticing her students' hesitation, she asked if they wanted to discuss the question as a whole class rather than in pairs. Students quickly agreed, and she shifted to a whole-class conversation first, so that her students were more comfortable with the definition and examples of an opinion. In contrast, sometimes it is important to spontaneously remove unnecessary scaffolding when you notice students do not need it. For example, if you notice that students do not need teacher or peer support to complete a task, you might ask students to engage in the activity or assignment independently.

Kendall's spontaneous scaffolding demonstrated important recognition of students' abilities and needs in the moment of instruction, and it allowed her to maintain high expectations and offer a challenging lesson by providing appropriate support specific to her learners.

Differentiation

All students need ways to engage with high-quality content so that they are able to succeed in school and beyond (e.g., Baecher et al., 2012; Haycock, 2001; MacGillivray & Rueda, 2003). However, multilingual students may need different ways of accessing that content. Andrew described differentiation this way:

> I'm trying to think, "What am I doing as an ESOL teacher to take this content and make it manageable, but still rigorous? Still challenging for these different groups who are at different levels?" It's a lot of processes coming together at once. Looking at students individually, "What's their level? What's their background?" On a macro level, "What is the district expecting from 2nd-graders? What should they be doing?" And then looking at the child outside of those things. Personality-wise, interest level, how does that affect what they're doing?

Differentiation is an important means for offering a variety of "ways in" to the lesson so that engaging in the learning process becomes more accessible for students (e.g., Tomlinson, 2014). According to Baecher and her colleagues

(2012), teachers should think carefully about multilingual students' strengths and challenges in English when differentiating for them, and use the same content objective for all students, while differentiating their language objective according to students' English language proficiency (for more on content and language objectives see the section below).

Differentiation can feel daunting, but you can keep it manageable by not trying to do everything at once. For example, Baecher and her colleagues (2012) note that one way to differentiate is to identify a "base activity" for students with higher proficiency in English and adjust the linguistic complexity for students with lower proficiency in English. Some teachers also start by creating the activity with a middle level of complexity and then identify how to make the activity both more and less linguistically demanding. You will need to try it to see what works well for you. In part, this depends on your context, including the number of students you have at a particular English proficiency level.

Differentiation is connected to both comprehensible input and scaffolding. Differentiating your instruction means selecting and implementing the right amount and kinds of comprehensible input and scaffolding for various groups or individual students, based on their abilities and needs. For instance, when learning about the life cycle of plants, the baseline activity might be to use a word bank to fill in key words in a paragraph, while students at a higher proficiency level in English might receive an assignment to write a few sentences about the plant life cycle, and students at a lower proficiency level might put images of the life cycle in the right sequential order.

Differentiation helps ensure that the tasks at hand align with students' existing knowledge and strengths, as well as help them continue to grow their language and content knowledge. Differentiation can occur in at least three ways, when teachers differentiate the content, process, and/or product (Tomlinson, 2003, 2014):

- Content—What a student needs to know and/or how the student will access that information
- Process—Activities the student engages in to make sense of or master new material
- Product—Vehicles through which students demonstrate and extend what they have learned

According to Tomlinson, teachers should also decide whether and what to differentiate based upon the following student characteristics: readiness, interests, and learning profile.

- Readiness—Students' entry point related to particular knowledge, understanding, or skills. When students have less readiness, they may benefit from more direct instruction or practice. When their readiness is more developed, they may need to skip the practice portion, or work at a brisker pace.

- Interests—Students' affinity, curiosity, or passion for a particular topic or skill. Bringing students' particular interests to bear on the content is an important part of their engagement. For instance, a student interested in women's history may more readily engage with a lesson on the U.S. Civil War if they can create a final project about the role of women in the war.
- Learning profile—The ways in which a student learns, which Tomlinson (2014) notes may be shaped by intelligence preferences, gender identity, culture, or learning style. Here we add that the learning profile may also be shaped by home languages, ways of engaging in literacy practices, and other culturally and linguistically mediated experiences.

We share examples of these differentiation methods in Table 3.1.

As Tomlinson (2014) helpfully summarizes, teachers can decide to adapt "one or more of the curricular elements (content, process, product) based on one or more of the student characteristics (readiness, interest, learning

Table 3.1. Differentiated Instruction

How instruction is differentiated (curricular elements)	Examples of differentiation based on student characteristics
Content	• reading materials on different levels (readiness) • vocabulary banks with a different number and difficulty of words (readiness) • choose which text to read about a topic (interests) • print text, audio, or video (learning profile, interests, readiness)
Process	• use manipulatives to support understanding of a concept (readiness) • allow more time on a task (readiness, learning profile) • choose three out of five tasks to complete related to the topic (interests, learning profile) • work alone, with a partner, or with a small group (learning profile, interests, readiness)
Product	• use different rubrics (readiness, learning profile) • different options for final product, such as puppet show, letter, mural (interests, readiness, learning profile) • create own assignment (interests) • create final product alone or with group (learning profile, readiness)

profile) at any point in a lesson or unit" (p. 19). Santamaría (2009) asserts that strong instruction for multilingual students also includes differentiating content, process, and product in culturally and linguistically responsive ways, and she notes that when teachers attend only to academic diversity in their differentiated instruction, they risk overlooking significant linguistic, cultural, and social factors that impact multilingual students' learning in complex ways. You might differentiate the content of a lesson by offering texts from different cultures; offering students various levels of linguistic scaffolds based on their proficiency (e.g., a sentence frame vs. a word bank); or having students choose what kind of an assessment they use to demonstrate their understanding.

Good differentiation requires clear and meaningful assessment. The teachers on our team were aware of this, as Chris noted:

> To start doing a better job of differentiating instruction for the highly variable needs of my students across my course load, I need to begin by identifying a few key categories of academic skills in which my students differ across all classes. This might include an analysis of basic reading and writing skills in their home language, their oral proficiency in English, and their ability to follow written and oral directions in English. I would use a combination of formal and informal assessments, such as anecdotal notes and short reading/writing assessments, to gauge proficiency in those areas. I would then create a spreadsheet to record and identify whether students in each class fit into groups based on proficiency levels, data that I could then use to plan differentiated instruction to target the needs of the different groups.

As we discuss in Chapter 5, you can best teach your students when you deeply understand what they already know, and what they need further support to learn. Instruction and assessment go hand in hand; they can continually inform and build upon each other.

Integrated Content and Language Objectives

A clear direction and purpose for lessons and units is another critical aspect of teaching multilingual students, and this often takes the form of well-conceived and interconnected content and language objectives. These objectives generally come from the curriculum standards that your school uses and should be something you can observe based on what students do during the lesson. Strong objectives support you and your students because they set clear expectations, allow for demanding and grade-appropriate learning, and foster the achievement of multilingual students. Writing good objectives is challenging, and many teachers focus only on their content objectives. However, when working with multilingual students you should consider both the content *and* the language that students are learning in lessons.

Importantly, you should consider the kind of language demands that the content of the lesson creates. Language demands are the kinds of language (for example, vocabulary, language structures, purposes, language domains such as reading or speaking, and language learning strategies) needed to participate in the lesson. One question you can ask yourself that will help you to identify language demands in your lesson is, "What language will students need to learn and use to accomplish the content objective?" When teachers examine the language demands of the content they are teaching and think carefully about both content and language objectives to guide their planning and assessment, there is greater likelihood that they will be successful at helping students learn both language and content in their lessons (Baecher et al., 2014). Additionally, when teachers explore the language demands in their lessons, and use those demands to inform their objective writing, multilingual students demonstrate higher achievement (Echevarría et al., 2008).

Many teachers tend to focus heavily on vocabulary in their language objectives, and they target speaking and writing more frequently than reading and listening. In contrast, they tend to give very little attention to language functions, or the different purposes for which we use language (such as comparing/contrasting, stating an opinion, classifying, asking permission, apologizing, evaluating, and many others; see, for instance, Hill & Miller, 2013), and to language learning strategies when they write language objectives (Baecher et al., 2014). Thus, an awareness of language demands beyond vocabulary is important for supporting multilingual students' language development in your lessons.

Teachers often find writing language objectives more challenging than writing content objectives, and it helps to engage in a lot of practice and view multiple examples to guide you. It is useful to write your objectives in student-friendly language and share them at the beginning of the lesson so students understand where the lesson is headed and why, as well as to revisit them at the end of the lesson to discuss what students have learned and what you will continue to work on together. Understanding the lesson's purpose and discussing the objectives at the beginning and end of the lesson as a routine go a long way toward helping students to feel at ease, understand the focal point and purpose of the lesson, and better comprehend the material. As Andrea explained: "Even if they don't fully absorb or digest the objective the first time, I think it's really helpful to give them that multiple exposure to the language of the objective, and also to understand the concept, put it in practice, and then come back to it, and say, 'Oh that's what I just did. That's starting to make a little more sense.'"

In Table 3.2, we share examples of content objectives, language objectives, and language demands from the teachers' lessons. Note that in these examples, elementary teachers use the first-person "I" to state objectives, and secondary teachers use the third-person "students."

Table 3.2. Content and Language Objectives

Teacher	Content objective	Language objective	Language demands
Erica	I can name community helpers.	Erica's lesson plan included two versions of the language objective, one for her, and a less linguistically complex one to share with her newcomer students. This was her objective: *I can speak and write my own sentences by using nouns and pronouns to identify community helpers with the support of sentence frames and pictures.* This was the objective she posted for students: *We will say and write different kinds of community helpers.*	• Language domains (speaking, writing) • Language functions (naming things) • Vocabulary (community helpers) • Language structures (pronouns, singular and plural nouns)
Kendall	I can identify problems and solutions in a text.	I can write a paragraph to explain the problems and solutions in the text with the support of a graphic organizer and a word bank.	• Language domains (writing, speaking) • Language functions (explaining, identifying problem and solution)
Andrea	I can answer "where" and "when" questions by adding details to my sentences.	I can use the preposition words on, at, and in to answer "where" and "when" questions in complete sentences, with the support of visuals and sentence frames.	• Language domains (writing) • Language functions (answering questions) • Vocabulary (on, at, in) • Language structures (prepositions, where and when questions)
TC	Students will identify the steps of the plant life cycle.	Students will write the steps of the plant life cycle.	• Language domains (writing) • Language functions (identifying) • Vocabulary (plant life cycle)

(continued)

Teacher	Content objective	Language objective	Language demands
Melissa	Students will form a group and work together to assign roles, establish expectations, and make a plan.	Students will speak and listen to their group members to make a plan for the task.	• Language domains (speaking, listening) • Language functions (discussing and persuading)

SEEING IT IN ACTION

Planning and enacting integrated content and language instruction that is humanizing is pivotal to your work and to your multilingual students' success. As we have discussed above, there are several parts that comprise planning and teaching lessons, and next we highlight examples from the classrooms of TC, Erica, and Nancy. These examples demonstrate how the teachers make their input more comprehensible to students, and how they support their instruction to make it meaningful, accessible, and appropriately challenging so that their students can learn the same content as their English-dominant peers. They humanize their instruction through high expectations accompanied by helpful supports that recognize their students as capable learners and meaningful contributors.

TC

TC is a secondary ESOL science teacher who teaches primarily 9th- and 10th-grade newcomer multilingual students. In the example below, she provides both comprehensible input and scaffolding when she instructs her students how to work with a partner in a dictation activity about what they learned from watching a video about photosynthesis.

> *TC:* You're going to share what you learned with a friend. We're going to do an interview, *una entrevista.* You're going to dictate. So, Adam, can you be my friend?
>
> *Adam:* Yes.
>
> *TC:* (To the class.) I'm going to ask him what did you *learn*? Adam, what did you learn from the video?
>
> *Adam:* I learned that . . .
>
> *TC:* (Modeling, reminding all students what will help their peers.) But wait, Adam, go slow, because English is new for me. So I'm going to write it down as you dictate. (Prompting the class to begin their dictation with the name of their partner.) So my friend's name, what's my friend's name?

Students: Adam.

TC: Adam. (Writes this down on projector screen.) So I'm going to say "Adam," and then what verb? Verb. *Verbo.*

Students pause and TC reminds them of the question, where the verb is found.

TC: What did Adam *learn?*

Students: Learned.

TC: So, he learned. "Adam learned." Adam please continue. "Adam learned. . . ."

Adam: What is photosynthesis.

TC: (Writing on projector.) "Adam learned what is photosynthesis." Can you give some more details?

Adam: Yes. The process help to work. . . .

TC: How what works?

Adam: Help the leaves absorb the water. And transfer to oxygen, to clean oxygen for the environment. . . .

TC: But remember Adam, your partner might have to ask you to repeat some things because some words are going to be a little difficult. But is Adam going to say, "Here Ms. Ellis, just copy?" (TC mimes handing her partner the completed work to copy, rather than listening to comprehend her partner's dictation.)

Adam: (Laughs.) No.

TC: No! He's going to just repeat some words. Your partner is going to say, "Wait, Adam! In English, how do you spell or how do you say this again?" Okay? So I'm going to give you guys five minutes. Find a friend at your table. You guys are going to interview that friend, and then that friend is going to interview you.

TC worked with Adam to demonstrate how the class members would engage with one another to discuss the video they had just watched about photosynthesis. She provided comprehensible input to students by acting out the process they would use in their pairs: by using repetition and restating key words and phrases; by placing emphasis on keywords; by pausing; by using Spanish (the home language of all the students in her class); and by slowing her rate of speech and encouraging students to remember to do this with their partners. TC was also making language learning strategies evident to her students by highlighting the importance of asking speakers to slow down and to repeat themselves. She also scaffolded her instruction by demonstrating how to do their pair work, making sure to emphasize how to engage and how not to engage in this activity successfully—not just copying from one another.

Additionally, TC provided a sentence starter, writing "(Student name) learned . . ." on the document camera. The opportunity for students to discuss what they learned with a peer was another form of scaffolding, by providing the opportunity to practice using key vocabulary about photosynthesis that they had learned in a prior lesson. She culminated this part of the lesson by asking students to highlight the key vocabulary that emerged in their partner's dictation to them, again reinforcing the important words and phrases in the unit.

TC's comprehensible input and scaffolding supported student learning of her content objective for the lesson, which was that students would be able draw and label a diagram demonstrating the process of photosynthesis. TC's practice was humanizing because it provided ways for students to engage with demanding content at an appropriate linguistic level so that they could be part of the conversation and learn grade-level material. She also positioned Adam as a competent model for his peers and built a classroom community around students' ability to teach and learn from one another.

Erica

Erica is an elementary ESOL teacher who teaches kindergarten and 2nd-grade students. In the example below, she teaches a pull-out math lesson about *more than*, *less than*, and *equal* to five kindergartners with beginning-level proficiency in English who speak Spanish at home. Pay attention to how Erica differentiates and scaffolds her instruction based upon the ways that learners respond to the lesson, and how she uses visual examples to provide comprehensible input.

> Erica places three colorful plastic blocks in front of herself and asks her students how many she has. Flora, who is still working on learning her number vocabulary, says: "Two." Samuel helps Flora saying: "Three," which Flora repeats.
>
> *Erica:* I have three blocks. I want you to show me more blocks. Show me more than three.
>
> All students take out more than three blocks.
>
> *Erica:* More than three?
> *Lucas:* One, two, three, four, five, six, I have six.
> *Erica:* Okay, now, help me count.
>
> Erica shows students a card with the word "more" written on it, with 11 blue dots and three red dots, and the blue dots circled. She says the word "more," and asks students to help her say it aloud together.

Students: More!

Erica: More! I have two groups right here. I have blue group and red group. Which group has more?

Students: Blue!

Erica: Blue! Okay. So, I have three blocks. Do you have more than I have?

Students: Yes.

Erica: All right, Flora, show us how many blocks you have.

Flora: Two. (She has six.)

Erica: (Helping Flora to adjust her number vocabulary.) How many? Let's count, can you count them for us?

Students, with Flora: One, two, three, four, five, six.

Erica: Six! She has six blocks. Friends, is six more than three?

Lucas: Yes!

Next, Erica takes out six blocks and places three in front of herself, and three in front of Liana.

Erica: Who has more?

Students giggle.

Lucas: You, and Liana, Liana, you.

Erica: Liana and me? Who has more?

Lucas: Nobody.

After asking the class how many blocks they each have, and students reply "Three," Erica explains that these are the same number, or equal.

Erica: If it's the same number, that means they're equal. Everybody say "equal."

After they practice with "equal," Erica moves on to the concept of "less." She tells her students that she has three blocks and she wants them to make less. She shows students a card with "less" written on it, with 11 blue dots and three circled red dots. Because they struggled a bit with the concept of "less" in their prior lesson, Erica also shows students some work they created in their last class with her: papers with two fishbowls and fish of five different colors, with numbers on each fishbowl. The paper has "I see . . ." printed twice, and students have completed the sentences by writing "more" or "less," and pasting a colored fish based on what is true for the fish pasted in the fishbowls. She asks Julia, Lucas, and Liana each to point to which fishbowl has less on their own papers. Next, she asks students to show her that they have less blocks than she does.

Samuel: One.

Flora: I have two.

Erica used at least three different kinds of visual representations to provide comprehensible input to students: blocks; cards with dots representing *more*, *less*, and *equal*; and colorful student-created paper fishbowls. All helped her to support student understanding of the concepts of "more/less than" and "equal to." Her repetition of key vocabulary and encouragement of students to repeat the key words was also an important comprehensible input strategy. Erica differentiated her instruction by providing more support during the process of applying "more/less than" and "equal to" based upon student readiness. For instance, when Erica asked students to take out more blocks than she had, Flora displayed more blocks but did not know the right word for "six." Erica differentiated for Flora by helping her count out loud, thus providing more number vocabulary to Flora, who clearly understood the concept of more. Because she knew her students had been challenged by the concept of "less," Erica also scaffolded for all class members by drawing on their own work as a model for "less than." As she explained, she used their fishbowl assignment to remind them of their prior work on these concepts:

> They loved doing this fishbowl thing, and it was a highly motivating activity for them. So, when some of them got confused with more and less, I could use their own work as scaffolding. Because then they see that it's not me telling them what they did wrong and saying "Here's how you do it right." Instead, it's like, well, "Here's what you did, you know how to do this, let's kind of break this down."

Like TC, Erica developed a supportive classroom environment that valued students as capable contributors with important knowledge to share. Erica's pedagogy was humanizing because she positioned students as knowledgeable by reminding them of their work in the previous lesson on "more" and "less." Rather than telling them they were wrong, or simply teaching them the definition of the word "less," she encouraged them to apply the "less than" concept from their fishbowl activity to their work with the blocks. In doing so, she reinforced their identities as competent learners.

Nancy

Nancy is an ELA teacher in an international high school that enrolls only multilingual students. Nancy's school groups students heterogeneously in terms of their language proficiency levels, and much of what students do is accomplished at their own pace. Therefore, on any given day, students are working at different places in the unit. In this example, Nancy is teaching an ELA unit about identity to her 9th- and 10th-grade students and engaging them in a lesson about characterization. Her content objective is for her students to characterize the speaker in Sandra Cisneros's short story *Eleven* by examining her actions, thoughts, words, and descriptions. Nancy's language objective is for her students to read and identify different forms of characterization by selecting quotations from the text and analyzing their meaning.

In the excerpt below, Nancy works with a newcomer student with low proficiency in English to read the short story, while some other groups read the story without her assistance. Look for how Nancy differentiates and scaffolds her instruction in this example:

> Nancy reads one word at a time and Anabela repeats after her: "You don't feel eleven. Not right away. It takes a few days, weeks even, sometimes even months before you say eleven when they ask you. And you don't feel smart eleven, not until you're almost twelve. That's the way it is." They finish reading the passage together.
>
> *Nancy:* You got it! Good job, right?
>
> When the other groups finish reading, Nancy explains the next part of the task, which is underlining sections of the text that provide evidence for characterizing the narrator, and then writing about that characterization. She shows the students what is expected by modeling on the document camera, and she shares two examples she had already done for the students and offers sentence starters to some students.

Nancy explained how she made decisions about what kind of support to provide students as she interacted with each one during the lesson:

> On a daily basis, I decide, based on what I observe as I am circulating the room, what some necessary scaffolds are, or what further differentiation is needed. I was reading to Anabela, one of our newcomers, and having her repeat. I do more one-on-one personalized levels of differentiation based on what I want each kid to experience. All the kids are engaging with the material and you see the different levels of differentiation, and I'm checking in with them on a one-on-one basis throughout the day, throughout the week. I have scaffolds in place, but I give students the content first and allow them to grapple with it, and then add the scaffolds in as I see fit.

Nancy differentiated the process for her students in this lesson. All students read the same content and would ultimately produce the same characterization sheet at the end, but the activities they engaged in to master the content (the process) varied based on their English language proficiency. She supported Anabela, a newcomer, by reading and interpreting the text with her. Other students with higher proficiency in English read the text and worked on interpreting it in their small groups. Nancy also differentiated her process by providing different levels of scaffolds, such as sentence starters, to students who needed them, based on their level of English language proficiency. She provided additional scaffolding with her examples of characterization shared on the document camera. Her practice was humanizing because all students were viewed as capable of engaging in demanding grade-level text, as long as they were appropriately supported in doing so. It was also humanizing because she trusted students to support one another in their groups, and to work at a pace that was appropriate for them, while also challenging them to work at the level of which they were capable.

TAKE ACTION IN YOUR CLASSROOM

- Use visual representations, repetition, emphasis on keywords, rephrasing, clear enunciation, and acting out to provide comprehensible input to your students. You can also include more pauses, use more high-frequency words, and make sure to include definitions of key words to support comprehensible input.
- You scaffold when you provide appropriate support to help learners increase their understanding of new material and move toward greater independence. You can both increase and decrease support based on what you discover about students' existing knowledge and skills. You can scaffold with individual supports, and you can also scaffold on a larger scale across a lesson, unit, or whole school year, by creating a planned progression in which you provide and then gradually remove support.
- Differentiated instruction provides variation in the content, process, or product of a lesson to support students' readiness, interest, or learning profile. Choose leveled texts, create math problems that require different levels of understanding, or offer science notes that have more or less of the content filled in, to create varying levels of content and process based on readiness. Offer students opportunities to choose what their topic or culminating product will be as a way to differentiate based on their interests. There are many ways to differentiate and you can begin to slowly incorporate these to keep things manageable.
- Make sure you create clear and integrated content and language objectives for your lesson. These objectives are based on the curriculum standards that your school uses and should be concrete

and specific enough that you can see whether students have reached them, either through their performance or product. To write your language objectives, think about the language demands that the content creates. Write your objectives in student-friendly language and share them with students so they know the purpose of the lesson. Discussing what you have done at the end of the lesson and how you have met lesson objectives also helps students to solidify their understanding of the lesson content.

QUESTIONS FOR REFLECTION

1. What might happen if a teacher does not provide comprehensible input in a lesson? How might students engage with the content? How might students behave if they cannot understand the lesson?
2. Think back to a skill you had to learn. What scaffolds helped you learn that skill? Can you provide a specific example of how you might want to scaffold in a lesson or a unit?
3. What do you think is the most challenging part of differentiating instruction? Are there some ways you think you can start doing this in your teaching that sound manageable to you?
4. Think of a lesson you have taught or observed recently. Can you identify a content objective and a language objective for that lesson? What language demands did the content of the lesson create? Try writing clear, student-friendly content and language objectives for that lesson.

CHAPTER 4

Language and Literacy Development

> Language encompasses a lot of things. There are all these little pieces that add up to make a whole. And all of those things are like tools in a toolbox. For students to be able to access the content they need all those tools. You can't build a house with just a hammer and a nail. I think it's important to think about how different those pieces might be in students' home languages. My job is to give them those different pieces of language and also show them how to use the pieces and put them together so that they can access the content.
>
> —Erica, elementary ESOL teacher

Erica shares how complex and nuanced language is, and she identifies many of the dimensions she thinks about when teaching multilingual students. Language and literacy development are a critical part of multilingual students' success in school. You want to consider not only students' development in English, but also students' resources in the other languages they speak, and the ways in which these shape who they are and how others view them, which in turn impact their feelings of acceptance and success at school (Mercuri, 2012; Wong & Grant, 2007).

As we noted in Chapter 3, knowing your students well plays an important part in designing the right kind of instruction for them. As we described in detail in Chapter 1, particularly important for supporting students' language and literacy development is to know as much as you can about students' language and literacy in both their home languages and English, so that you can leverage and further strengthen their language and literacy development through your instruction (Hopewell, 2011; Pacheco & Miller, 2016). Furthermore, literacy is an important key to students' success across all content areas, and the disciplinary literacy demands and norms of different content areas require all of us to be adept in different kinds of reading and writing, as well as listening and speaking (Bunch et al., 2012; Fang & Coatoam, 2013).

DIMENSIONS OF SUPPORTING LANGUAGE AND
LITERACY DEVELOPMENT

In this chapter, we will discuss how teachers' engagement in this core practice helps them to support multilingual students' language and literacy development in ways that are responsive and humanizing. Fostering students' language and literacy development includes use of the following techniques:

- Promoting vocabulary development
- Using students' home language knowledge as a resource
- Engaging students in receptive and productive language use at various levels (word, sentence, and discourse levels)
- Adapting instruction based on awareness of the complexity of language and students' language development needs

Vocabulary development and use of a student's home language as a resource support comprehension, access to meaning, and participation in lessons. Focusing on receptive (listening and reading) and productive (speaking and writing) language use helps to develop students' skills for school participation, engagement, and success. Through it all, your awareness of the complexity of language will help you to appropriately adapt instruction in ways that support students' language development needs. These ways of supporting your multilingual students in developing language and literacy skills are a crucial way to humanize your teaching practice, as they are essential for students' full participation in school and society.

Promoting Vocabulary Development

Vocabulary is a central building block for language use. In fact, research on English-dominant students shows that by the time they are 6 years old, they usually recognize about 10,000 words (Law et al., 2017). By 8th grade, students should have a reading vocabulary of 25,000 words, and by 12th grade they should have a reading vocabulary of 50,000 words (Graves, 2006). Some researchers have estimated that from 3rd grade onward, this means that students should learn 2,000–3,000 new words per year (Nagy & Scott, 2000). While figures for multilingual students depend on a variety of factors, we know that vocabulary knowledge is strongly related to reading comprehension and academic success, and multilingual students are a subgroup that especially benefits from strong vocabulary support (Kinsella, 2005; Lehr et al., 2005).

It is important to make sure you are examining and using a wide range of vocabulary with your students. Isabel Beck and her colleagues have categorized words as belonging to three tiers (Beck et al., 2013). Tier 1 includes words students use every day; Tier 2 includes more complex, high-frequency words that are used in a variety of content areas; and Tier 3 words are discipline-specific vocabulary that are rarely used. These researchers urge teachers to focus their vocabulary instruction efforts most heavily on Tier 2 words because they are of high utility in multiple content areas (e.g., words like *demonstrate, coincidence, absurd*), whereas students have regular and frequent exposure to Tier 1 words (e.g., *girl, swim, warm*) and typically need less instruction in them. They also suggest that Tier 3 words be taught as the need arises, because they are topic- and domain-specific and used frequently only in particular content areas (e.g., *respiration, protagonist, amendment*).

Here are some important guidelines for deciding which words to focus on with your students:

- Importance and utility—How frequently is the word used?
- Instructional potential—Does the word build connections to other words and concepts?
- Conceptual understanding—Does knowing this word help build understanding and specificity? (Beck et al., 2005)

Additionally, repeated exposure to new words and phrases in a variety of contexts also supports multilingual students' learning of vocabulary. Some research shows that multilingual students need more than 10 encounters with a new word before they can remember what it means and use it themselves (Uchihara et al., 2019). Furthermore, reading both deeply (about a particular topic or in a particular content area) and broadly (across many topics or content areas) at an appropriately challenging level (students should be able to understand 90–95% or more of the text) also supports multilingual students in learning new vocabulary (Grabe, 2009; Schmitt et al., 2011).

Teachers should be aware of vocabulary and other language demands (see Chapter 3) in grade-level content. This awareness of the dual demands of content and language can be helpful for challenging multilingual students while also drawing on their linguistic resources and building new abilities. One way to use this awareness is to preview and practice vocabulary with multilingual students so that they feel confident and ready to discuss the new material together with their English-dominant peers. A focus on vocabulary development is humanizing because it gives students important access to rigorous and challenging content.

There are many strategies for supporting multilingual students' vocabulary growth in all of their languages:

- Checking students' knowledge of a word when it is first introduced
- Asking students if they know how to say a word in their home language and identifying cognates (words in two different languages that have a similar meaning, spelling, and pronunciation, such as telephone in English, and *teléfono* in Spanish)

- Examining the meaning of common prefixes (such as *re-, un-, non-, pre-, anti-*), suffixes (such as *–less, -ly, -ful, -ness*), and Greek and Latin root words that are common in English (such as *photo-, -ology, -graph*)
- Discussing how a word or word part is similar to another word students have learned or know
- Identifying multiple parts of speech for a new word (for example, *length*, a noun, and *long*, the related adjective)
- Using word walls or charts with key words on them, leaving them up as resources, and encouraging students to use and revisit these words in their speaking and writing
- Connecting a physical movement, tangible object, or visual image to represent a word (see Chapter 3)
- Sharing audio clips of the translation of new words in students' home languages—a strategy you can easily use if you do not speak students' home languages but want to provide the translation
- Using surrounding words and context to determine the meaning of a new word
- Creating personal dictionaries with the word in English, their home language, a definition, and a picture or other visual representation

Teachers also pay close attention to various meanings of new vocabulary and help students notice clues from text and pictures that might assist them in discerning the meaning. For instance, in a lesson in which students were reading a story with the verb "cry" in it, Andrew talked with his students about the particular meaning of the word "cry" in the text, making sure to distinguish the act of crying when sad or happy from the use of "cry" as a term for shouting. He helped them to arrive at this difference by looking at the pictures in the text, as well as the punctuation. His students noticed the use of an exclamation point and decided it meant that the character was yelling.

It is also important to note that vocabulary is a very important part of supporting multilingual students' language development, but vocabulary is only a part of what multilingual students need to learn, as we discuss further in the section about the complexity of language.

Using Students' Home Language Knowledge as a Resource

There are many academic, cognitive, communicative, and affective benefits to the maintenance of students' home languages, and to using them as much as you can as a resource in your teaching (Baker & Wright, 2017; Fox et al., 2019; Valdés et al., 2004). Long-standing research has shown that over time, and with strong bilingual instruction, students who are learning English can match or outperform their peers on academic tests in English across the curriculum (Collier, 1995; Thomas & Collier, 1997). Additionally, studies have shown that students who speak more than one language are more cognitively flexible, can draw from their knowledge of multiple languages at once, have stronger literacy capabilities, increased standardized test scores, enhanced creativity, and stronger memory, among several other benefits (Bialystok, 2011; Fox et al., 2019).

Of course, most students do not have access to fully bilingual instruction, but there are nevertheless ways to use your students' home languages as a resource in the classroom. For instance, if students who speak a language that shares cognates with English—such as Spanish—understand that recognizing those cognates can support their comprehension of English, they are better able to make use of that strategy successfully (Jiménez et al., 1996). Thus, it is helpful to highlight the important role of students' home languages in their academic progress and support them in as many ways as you can.

Acknowledging students' home languages is also supportive of students' cultural and linguistic identities (see Chapter 2). Think about how important your language use is to communicating and connecting with your family and community. Many of the ways you use language connect you to loved ones and to other groups to which you belong. There are ways of saying things and certain phrases that make it clear that you belong to particular groups (Gee, 2015), and you probably have words and phrases that are especially meaningful to you and other group members, whether these words and phrases come from a song, a book, a show, social media, a shared experience, or elsewhere.

When our languages are respected and valued, we also feel respected and valued as individuals. The connection between our language use and our identity and sense of worth is very important to each of us. For students who come to school speaking more than one language, it is therefore especially critical that we value all the other languages they speak. For instance, as we described in Chapter 2, it should be accepted as natural and valuable when students can translanguage, or move naturally between multiple languages to express themselves. Your classroom should make this possible through its norms and daily interactions.

Chris explained why he uses Spanish with his secondary students who speak Spanish at home, noting how challenging it can be for students to hear only English all day, and the importance of his support of their home languages as they also strive to learn English:

> I can feel students' intense frustration, having to take seven periods a day in English. It just makes it that much more difficult. I really use a lot of Spanish because I think it's unfair that we put them in that situation, and I think that we're stifling them intellectually. I don't hesitate to use the language resources that I have to help them engage with content because I think they seek out the teachers who will help them understand things because they're so frustrated.

There are many ways to position and draw upon students' home languages as a resource in your classroom. One is providing home language support as Chris describes, if you speak the students' home language. However, it is not necessary—and often not possible—to speak your students' home languages in order to use them as a resource in your teaching, especially if there are many different home languages represented in your school setting. You can still engage in the culturally and linguistically sustaining pedagogy we describe in Chapter 2, as well as offer multilingual texts and other resources in your classroom and encourage parents and caregivers to use their home languages with students so that you can continue developing their home language literacy together.

Engaging Students in Receptive and Productive Language Use

It is critical to make sure you give sufficient opportunities for multilingual students to engage in receptive (listening and reading) and productive (speaking and writing) language use, because all language users need to engage with both language input and language output (Krashen, 1985; Swain, 1985). It is also crucial to make sure you are working on receptive and productive language use at multiple levels of complexity—not only at the word level, but also receptive and productive modalities at the sentence level, and beyond (paragraph, page, entire text).

This does not mean that each domain of language requires equal time or that they need to be taught separately. In school settings, we often tend to emphasize reading and writing skills, but for students who are not just learning new content but also new language, it is important also to have many opportunities to speak and listen. For instance, content area classrooms frequently require reading and writing assignments, but multilingual students need opportunities to say and hear new words and phrases that are unfamiliar to them so that they can gain confidence in their pronunciation, understanding, and use (Fredricks & Peercy, 2020; Walqui & Heritage, 2018). Oral language skills are also an important support for students' developing literacy skills in English, allowing students to deepen their vocabulary, learn to pose questions, and use language learning strategies effectively (Saunders & O'Brien, 2006).

However, in other cases, multilingual students might not get enough practice with meaningful and extensive writing, and can feel anxiety about academic writing in English (Scullin & Baron, 2013), so sometimes more time needs to be spent there. In other words, it is important to be aware of what language skills students receive ample opportunities to practice in your classroom and other classrooms (see Chapter 6), and of what their experiences and backgrounds include (see Chapter 1), and to use evidence from formal and informal assessments (see Chapter 5) to help you identify where they would benefit from more practice. See Table 4.1 for examples of what you might do to support students' receptive and productive language use.

Table 4.1. Suggestions for Practicing Receptive and Productive Language Use

Language domains	Language proficiency level	Example activities
Speaking and listening	Newcomer, beginning	Pronounce and repeat new words and phrases several times together to help students gain confidence in how to say a new word; remind students that it is okay to make mistakes.
Speaking and listening	Newcomer, beginning	Structure opportunities for students' responses by first asking those students who are more confident and more likely to understand how to respond to questions or prompts; they can serve as models to help other students feel more confident in how to respond.
Reading and listening	Newcomer, beginning, intermediate	Project or share text with key words in it and work together to help students identify those words by circling, underlining, or highlighting them so that they start to recognize what the words look and sound like.
Reading and speaking	Newcomer, beginning	Give students opportunities to read aloud with fluency (accuracy and appropriate speed) and appropriate expression; start by modeling this for them.
Reading	Beginning, intermediate	Read a text and identify particular details (such as main idea, supporting ideas, key facts).
Speaking and listening	Intermediate and advanced	Have students work in small groups or pairs and then report back on their main ideas to the whole class after their small group work.
Writing	Intermediate and advanced	Model the parts and writing of a paragraph.
Speaking	All levels	Use a tactile item like popsicle sticks or clothespins with students' names on them to keep track of whether you are hearing from each student during class. Alternatively, give students tokens or chips that they should try to "use up" during class by offering a response or idea.
Speaking and listening	All levels	Brainstorm together first as a group before beginning a task so that students feel more confident about the language and ideas they will use to complete the task.

(continued)

Table 4.1. Suggestions for Practicing Receptive and Productive Language Use (*continued*)

Language domains	Language proficiency level	Example activities
Speaking, listening, writing	All levels	Gather peers' opinions, ideas, or experiences around a particular topic, and then report them back verbally and/or in writing. This can include filling out a bingo-type card when students can find classmates that have specific characteristics or experiences (for example: "has been to the beach," "has an older sister," or "loves to read").
Speaking, listening, reading, writing	All levels	Assign different roles in small groups that require each student to engage with the language, the content, and one another (e.g., a recorder, a reporter, a task manager, an equipment manager).
Speaking or writing	All levels	Find an intriguing visual image and ask students to describe what they think is going on in the image (what a person is thinking or doing, what just happened, what is about to happen).
Writing	Newcomers, beginners	Have students copy letters/words, use pictures to supplement their writing, or construct their own simple sentences depending on the student's literacy level.
Writing	All levels	Examine and discuss models of good writing.

Adapting Instruction to Students' Language Development Needs

In this section we focus on the fact that language is complex and has many dimensions. Teaching language is not just about teaching vocabulary words. As Erica pointed out at the beginning of the chapter, language is like a set of tools in a toolbox, and there are many different ways we use it and there are different ways we need to help multilingual students understand how to use it. These tools include both smaller and bigger parts of language, for example: introducing students to the sounds and system of sounds that are possible (such as, what does *ch* sound like?); the ways that words are put together to make particular meanings (such as prefixes/suffixes/root words, and the use of past tense *-ed* verb endings in English); word order in sentences (such as the common subject-verb-object structure in English), and how we indicate respect or deference or close ties through our language use (such as through the use of polite requests or ways of addressing someone).

An important part of your work is balancing the complexity of language and students' developmental language needs alongside recognition of students as valued and capable classroom members. Multilingual students come to the classroom with a host of resources, including their background knowledge *in* English and in their home language, and their metalinguistic knowledge *about* English and their home language (see Chapter 1). When you can value and leverage students' existing assets while also teaching the different "tools" and foundational aspects of literacy in English that relate to the content they are learning, you are helping contribute to students' academic success.

It is also important to remember that students will develop their understanding of language and their literacy skills at different rates. Students who speak a home language with a similar alphabet, syntax (word order), text directionality, and other features of language and literacy that are similar to English will more easily be able to find meaning in English (see Chapter 1). Having appropriate expectations for what students can understand, produce, and do in English, given their current proficiency in English and background in their home language and schooling, is also important. These features will have an impact on how complex students find the language you are using, and the kinds of language development needs that they have.

Multilingual students are resource rich and come to your classroom with prior knowledge and linguistic skills, so make room for recognizing and capitalizing on them. For instance, pay attention to whether students might already understand a concept and just need the right English phrases for it. Doing brief, informal check-ins as you discuss a new topic will allow you to determine whether students need help with the concept or simply the language (see Chapter 5) for expressing the concept. Furthermore, scaffolding new content and language to support students based on what you know about their background knowledge will also help them to grasp more complex language and will allow you to be responsive to their resources and needs for language support (see Chapters 1 and 3). When possible, think about how you can reorganize content in ways that go from more personally meaningful to more abstract. If you are working on reading and writing particular genres of text with your students, starting with narratives will allow them a more concrete entry point, and then you can build to more abstract texts, such as news articles, reference texts (like encyclopedias), historic documents, and other informational text.

For teachers who are teaching a particular sheltered content course specifically for multilingual students (such as ESOL biology), or just focusing on specific content in a unit, this creates the additional demand of the complexity of the content, and teachers need to be well versed in both the vocabulary and other structures that the content requires, and how to convey that to students (see Chapter 3; see also Hyland, 2007; Rose & Martin, 2012; Turkan et al., 2014). For instance, if you are teaching math word problems, you will need to make sure that students understand the math concepts, and the words and meaning of those concepts, but also any vocabulary that is part of the word problem itself, and any specific cultural understanding those word problems might require. Erica noted that teaching a math problem about flower beds could present a challenge for her multilingual students who were from a context where flower beds might not be common. Therefore, the complexity of what you are doing is also driven by the content and the ways in which language gets used to make meaning in, with, and from that content (Brisk, 2015, Derewianka & Jones, 2016).

SEEING IT IN ACTION

Supporting language and literacy development is a critical part of all academic instruction, and it is particularly important for multilingual students because they are learning and developing these skills in an additional language, English. Their home languages may or may not be similar to English, and their literacy in their home languages will vary depending on numerous factors, including their prior schooling and how their home languages are used at home and in their communities. Their home languages also represent a foundational part of their identity and the ways in which they connect with loved ones at home and in their community. Creating opportunities to value, develop, and sustain students' linguistic and cultural resources through the use of translanguaging and classroom materials in students' home languages (see Chapter 2), as well as providing high-quality opportunities to develop multilingual students' language and literacy in English, are important aspects of humanizing practice in your classroom and school settings. Below we highlight examples from TC and Kendall's classrooms, which demonstrate how they support students' vocabulary development, receptive and productive language skills, use their home language as a resource, and adapt their instruction in ways that recognize both the complexity of language and students' language development needs. They humanize their instruction through their careful attention to ways of developing students' language and literacy that will support students' learning, using, and thriving in English.

TC

In the following secondary ESOL biology lesson, notice how TC focuses on using students' home language as a resource, and also on engaging students in receptive and productive language use and vocabulary development. Also pay attention to the Tier 3 words in this lesson, which students need to know to participate in biology content.

> TC's biology lesson is for 9th-grade Spanish-speaking newcomers with new content about energy transfer, including information about producers, consumers, and decomposers, and types of ecological relationships. She begins, as she always does, by introducing key vocabulary. She pronounces each of the 18 new words, and students repeat them after her twice, to get more comfortable with how to say each word. TC reminds students in both English and Spanish that the final letter *e* in English

words like carnivore and herbivore are silent, helping the students to know not to pronounce that letter as they learn the new words (*e* is never silent in their home language, Spanish).

After TC models for the class, students write down their new words, and then work in their assigned groups on writing definitions, using sentence frames that TC provides. They use information from their notes and their textbook to help them complete their definitions. For homework, they will write the definition of these new vocabulary words in their home language and draw a picture that represents the definition, and in their next class meeting they will identify and highlight these new words in sentences. Later, students will use these new words in more extended receptive and productive language: first, answering questions in complete sentences about energy transfer; then writing an essay that has sentence frames; and finally completing and presenting a project to their classmates about energy transfer.

TC explained how important language, and especially learning and using new vocabulary, is for succeeding in her ESOL biology class:

> For vocabulary development, we have to hit all four domains. We have to hit it in listening, reading, writing, and speaking. On the first day we look at new vocabulary—even if we don't know the definition, let's first just be able to say it. Let's repeat it individually, let's repeat as a whole group. Let's all hear it and then write it. So it's all of those domains. And then we get into the definitions because it can be overwhelming to see all of these words around a word that's supposed to be important. The second day, being able to at least highlight the word that we're learning about among all of these other words, and find the one that we're trying to learn in this topic. I try to take my time with it and not overwhelm the students. Because science has a lot of vocabulary, I also provide a lot of visuals and I have the students draw their own visual reference representations for each word.

TC supported language and literacy development in several ways in this lesson. She supported students' vocabulary development through multiple approaches. First, she tried to ensure that students were comfortable pronouncing new words. She used students' home language knowledge as a resource when she used both Spanish and her knowledge *of* Spanish to highlight a feature of pronunciation that is different in English than in Spanish (silent *e* in English). She encouraged students to use Spanish as one of their ways of defining the new words. TC also ensured that there were opportunities to practice both receptive and productive language, at the word level and at the sentence and paragraph level, when students said the new words aloud, then identified them in writing. Students further developed vocabulary by writing the words and their definitions, and this eventually led to working with paragraphs in which they read sentence frames TC created and they inserted key vocabulary where it belonged. This all culminated in group oral presentations about energy transfer to their classmates, in which they used the key vocabulary to share what they had learned. TC's pedagogy was humanizing because she was focusing on what students can do and achieve with their existing linguistic resources, as well as providing them strategies for accessing new discipline-specific vocabulary and content.

Kendall

Kendall engages in a number of ways to support students' language and literacy development in a lesson on cause and effect with seven 3rd-grade multilingual students who have intermediate proficiency in English. Pay special attention to the way she adapts her instruction to the complexity of language and students' language development needs, as well as how she supports students' receptive and productive language skills. Cause and effect are particularly challenging for students to understand, because chronologically the cause occurs first, but sometimes we describe the effect first, as Kendall is careful to help her students understand.

> *Kendall:* So I have two pictures. (She places a picture of a banana peel and a picture of someone slipping on a chart.) You're going to talk to your partner: Which one is the cause, which one is the effect, and how do you know?

> Students discuss the pictures in small groups, and when Kendall brings them back to the whole-class discussion, Gabriel raises his hand to speak.

> *Gabriel:* The effect is that the banana peel was on the floor. The cause is that I slipped on it.
> *Kendall:* So you think that it's like this? (She switches the order of the pictures, placing the slipping picture on the left and the banana picture on the right of the chart.) Okay, Jade, what do you think?
> *Jade:* I disagree with Gabriel. I think it's the other way around. I forgot their names. The banana goes first, and then the slip goes there (pointing to the right).
> *Gabriel:* I get it now!
> *Carmen:* I disagree with Gabriel because I think the cause . . . is the banana.
> *Gabriel:* I accidentally mixed up the words.
> *Kendall:* That's okay! We're just learning. All right, so, how did you guys know which one comes first? What do you think? Patricia?
> *Patricia:* He dropped the banana on the floor first.
> *Kendall:* Okay, Larry dropped the banana, and Gabriel slipped. If we were going to put them on the timeline, do you think that Larry dropped the banana should go before or after Gabriel slipped?

Students: Before.
Kendall: (Pointing to the left side of the chart.) So like here?

Some students say yes, and some say no.

Kendall: So, wait, could I say Gabriel slipped at lunch, and then Larry
dropped the banana peel?

Multiple students think this doesn't make sense.

Zaida: How could Gabriel fall right now, but Larry hasn't dropped the
banana peel? How could he fall when nothing was in the way?
Kendall: All right. Yeah, I agree. So you guys are saying that when we're
doing cause and effect, the cause has to come first in the timeline.
Do you agree?
Students: Yes.
Kendall: Yeah. The cause has to come first. Because it's the thing that
makes the effect happen, so it has to come first. So if I wanted to
join these two events together, into one big 3rd-grade sentence, do
you think that I should put the word because over here, with the
effect, or should I put because with the cause?

Students give different answers.

Kendall: So, would you guys say that the word "because" needs to stick
together with the cause in your sentence?
Franklin: Gabriel slipped at lunch because Larry dropped . . . Uh, yeah.
Kendall: Yeah! I agree, we want to make sure that we use the word
"because." It always sticks together with the cause in your sentence.

After giving students an opportunity to discuss and practice with cause
and effect, Kendall gives each student a picture of either a cause or an
effect. They need to find their partner with the corresponding picture
(for example, a picture of falling rain as the cause pairs with growing
flowers as the effect), and then put their pictures in the appropriate cause
or effect column in the pocket chart. After all the pictures are placed,
students share their sentences. Although students have cause and effect
correctly placed in the pocket chart, they need support with putting the
cause and effect into a sentence frame using "because," and Kendall
helps them.

Carmen: The cause is the rain because the rain is falling down, and the
flowers starting to grow.
Kendall: Okay, so the flowers are growing because the rain is falling.

Jade: (Trying her sentence next.) The girl ate too much candy because, uhh . . .

Kendall: I see what's tricky. When you make your sentences, start with your effect, so listen to mine. He slipped on the banana peel because . . .

Jade: Ohh. . . .

Kendall: Try it out.

Jade: She got a cavity because she ate the candy.

Kendall: Excellent. Let me hear from Gabriel.

Gabriel: The girl blowed the bubble gum too big, wait . . . The gum popped because she blew it too big.

Kendall observed that it was challenging for students to identify cause and effect in a sentence, and that the use of language to describe cause and effect is complex. Although the cause occurs first chronologically, when written in a sentence using "because," the effect often comes first, and the cause follows it. Her attention to these details in her lesson supported students' vocabulary development so that they learn the labels "cause" and "effect" (Jade and Gabriel both noted at the beginning of the lesson that they were learning these English words), as well as the word "because" and its use and placement in the sentence. Her support of their understanding of the concepts of cause and effect was carefully scaffolded (see Chapter 3) and gave students opportunities to practice receptive and productive language as they discussed cause and effect, listened to their partners, listened to their classmates explain cause and effect, and read aloud cause-and-effect sentences with the word "because." Her practice in this lesson was humanizing because she built respect and trust with her students, while also incorporating the academic rigor of complex language use. Her students felt comfortable admitting when they did not know words, or had made an error, and she made this a natural part of the learning process. Her lesson also offered students a deeper conceptual understanding of cause and effect, and support for how to linguistically represent cause and effect, which is common and important across many content areas. This understanding will help them to more fully participate in other lessons about cause and effect.

TAKE ACTION IN YOUR CLASSROOM

- Use the same graphic organizers to support receptive and productive language use schoolwide; the consistent use and appearance of specific graphic organizers will help multilingual students feel more confident and give them consistent practice and understanding of their purpose.
- Use concrete descriptions of what students at different levels of English proficiency can accomplish (such as the WIDA Can-Do Descriptors) to inform your teaching of reading, writing, speaking, and listening, and the ways that you support and develop them

in your classroom. Some teachers even share student-friendly descriptions with students and discuss with them what they need to do to "level up," or to move to the next level of proficiency and ability in a particular language domain. It is especially helpful if you accompany the level-up descriptions with activities and supports that foster participation at the next level.

- Make your students aware of different text structures (such as cause and effect, problem and solution, compare and contrast, and sequence) and the ways that they work; sharing this explicitly will support them in recognizing these when they read, and using them effectively in their writing.
- Color-code different parts of writing in a paragraph (topic sentence, supporting sentences, conclusion) to help students see the different pieces that comprise a paragraph. Support their recognition and practice of each kind of sentence, and work on composing paragraphs that have those components.
- Show models of what you expect students to produce, or how you expect them to interact, when they engage in receptive and productive language use in your class. Remember all the different language parts of what you're asking students to do, and make sure they are comfortable with each part (such as tense, subject-verb agreement, punctuation, key vocabulary, correct pronouns, pronunciation).

QUESTIONS FOR REFLECTION

1. What do you think are some of the most, and the least, effective ways you have learned new vocabulary? How would you apply these experiences to the ways in which you want to incorporate vocabulary instruction in your teaching?
2. Imagine going to school in a country where you don't know the language. Your teacher begins a lesson in a language that you don't know. However, you discover your teacher has some knowledge of English and some of your new schoolmates are fellow English speakers. You also have access to the Internet. What could your teacher do to help you learn the new language while tapping into your knowledge of English?
3. If you have students in your class who need practice with listening skills in English, what are some different ways you could offer opportunities to develop those skills?
4. What is linguistically complex about the instructional materials and activities in the content area(s) you teach? What supports can you put in place to help students tackle the challenges with the language and literacy skills embedded in your instruction?

CHAPTER 5

Assessment

At the end of the year, I always acknowledge where every student has grown. Every student knows that I see at least one positive thing. And every quarter we do a self-reflection where one of the questions is, "What is one thing I did well during this quarter?" Some kids will be like, "I didn't do anything well," and I'll remind them, "You know that one day when you came in and you read the warm-up? You did that super well. Just imagine back in September, you wouldn't have even tried to do it. You're acknowledged and I saw your growth."

—TC, secondary ESOL teacher

As TC explains, assessment is an important part of documenting student growth, and showing students their achievements as well as determining what they have learned is an important part of teaching multilingual students who are often unsure of where they stand with their language development, and school success in general. Assessment can be defined as "all those activities . . . that provide information to be used as feedback to modify teaching and learning activities" (Black & Wiliam, 2010, p. 82). Common assessment types that teachers use include the following:

- Formative assessments, or informal assessment activities, designed to collect "evidence [that] is actually used to adapt the teaching to meet student needs" (Black & Wiliam, 2010, p. 82). Formative assessments are often designed by teachers and may also be called classroom assessments. These can include rubrics, portfolios, exit tickets, homework, presentations, and many other ways of exploring what students have learned and still need more support with.
- Summative assessments, or more formal assessments, which "are generally conducted at the end of a unit, semester, or course to determine how much students know for the purpose of grading, certification, evaluation of progress, or for researching the effectiveness of a program or curriculum" (Box, 2019, p. 13). Summative assessments can be designed by teachers, but many instructional materials also contain ready-to-use summative assessments such as unit tests.

- Standardized assessments are often designed or adopted by a local or state education agency, distributed to schools and school districts to be used to measure student progress toward local, state, or national standards, and are often conducted on a large scale with high-stakes impacts on school staffing and funding.

DIMENSIONS OF ASSESSMENT

In this chapter, we discuss the ways you can attend to aspects of assessment for multilingual students, and the ways appropriate assessment can lead to humanizing pedagogy through:

- Designing and using both formal and informal assessments for language and content
- Interpreting the results of standardized tests, including English language proficiency tests
- Differentiating formal and informal assessments appropriate to students' language development and content knowledge

Assessment is an integral part of the planning-instruction-assessment cycle. The skills and knowledge teachers need to have and use in assessing students can also be called assessment literacy (Xu & Brown, 2016). Designing and using both formal and informal assessments to match content and language objectives are central parts of assessment literacy for teachers of multilingual students because of the need to accurately and fairly measure students' language and content knowledge—two connected but distinct areas. When teachers are inexperienced at assessing multilingual students, they may mistake a lack of English proficiency for a lack of content knowledge—or worse, a lack of talent, intellect, or motivation. This may lead to misinformed decisions about student instruction, course placement, and need for services such as literacy interventions (Bailey & Carroll, 2015).

It is equally important that you can accurately interpret the results of standardized tests and other formal assessments, which often carry even higher stakes. It is well documented that standardized assessments may be culturally and linguistically biased in either their content or the way they are administered (Hernandez, 1994; Siegel, 2014), which means that it is important to carefully consider how their results are used. For example, studies have shown that multilingual students are both under- and over-represented in special education (Chamberlain, 2005; Counts et al., 2018), partially due to inaccuracies in the identification and assessment processes. A so-called "do no harm" principle in assessment means that "students and their families should be protected from harmful personal impact of [the] assessment process and its consequences" (Rasooli et al., 2018, p. 171), such as a misidentification for special education.

When possible, assessments should be differentiated according to students' abilities. As Fairbairn and Jones-Vo (2010) point out, "in most cases, the standards-based content or topic (from the curriculum) must remain the same at all levels of language proficiency" (p. 83). Differentiating, then, means "adjusting the language-based expectations . . . and providing the necessary scaffolding and support" (p. 85) for students to complete the assessment.

This is crucial for humanizing the assessment of multilingual student performance because of the serious consequences that mistakes in assessment can carry for the student. However, when done accurately, fairly, and effectively, with sensitivity toward students as whole human beings, assessments allow teachers to help students rise to their fullest educational potential because they can help teachers know what students are capable of, and they can increase students' confidence in reaching their goals (Bartolomé, 1994). We examine each of these dimensions of humanizing assessment for multilingual students in more detail in the sections that follow.

Designing and Using Formal and Informal Assessments

Designing and using both formal and informal assessments are important parts of the decision-making you do as a teacher. For example, Andrew, an elementary ESOL teacher, used a running record, a type of assessment in which a teacher listens to a student read aloud and the teacher jots down words read correctly per minute as well as any errors (for a helpful article on the use of running records, see Barone et al., 2020). Andrew explained how this assessment impacted his lesson planning for his elementary-aged multilingual students:

> It usually starts as a running record, so I'll just check off to show how many words a minute they read correctly, and if they don't read something correctly, I'll code it, like, Janelle was able to say "sur," and "prise," but didn't do it all together (surprise), and Steven kept repeating things, like "go" instead of "get." Then I'll look to see if there are any skills or decoding of certain parts of words that's challenging. Like two weeks ago, I noticed that a lot of them were struggling with suffixes, so word work last week was a lot on suffixes and getting them to read the whole word. I use it to also just be aware of what they're doing really well and what they might need more support in.

As Andrew describes, assessment can give you an idea of what support students will need, as well as what students are already doing well—information you can use to guide your subsequent lesson planning.

In Chapter 3, we discussed planning integrated content and language objectives for each lesson. Here, we discuss how to assess student performance in ways that match the lesson's content and language objectives. A helpful metaphor is to think of objectives and assessments as a pair of matching bookends that hold up your instruction. When designing assessments, you should start with a look at your objectives, and ask yourself these questions:

- What do I want students to achieve with content by the end of this lesson?
- What do I want students to achieve with language by the end of this lesson?
- How do I measure whether students achieved these objectives?

This process of looking at the end goals of your lesson first and then working backward to plan the activities that will get students there is sometimes called backward design (Wiggins & McTighe, 2005). It is important to note that assessing content and language do not need to be separate processes, just as your instruction does not need to address content and language separately, but in an integrated manner. This makes sense since content standards include discipline-specific language that students need to master to learn and show understanding of the content (Hakuta, 2014). However, you do need to make sure that the language you are using to assess content knowledge is clear and comprehensible to your students, so that you are not inadvertently testing their language when you intend to examine their understanding of content.

In Table 5.1 are two examples of lesson objectives and the matching assessments from Erica's elementary and Melissa's high school classes. Note how the assessment addresses both the content and language objectives, and that the teachers use formative assessment tools they have developed.

When you design assessments, it's also important to consider whether students know *how* to show their knowledge and skills on the assessment. Multilingual students who are new to U.S. schools may not be familiar with the classroom tasks or tools that are commonly used as assessments, and modeling their use multiple times is important. For example, many teachers use a KWL chart as a form of pre- and post-assessment. In this chart, students write down things they already Know and Want to know about a topic (before reading or learning about the topic), and what they Learned about the topic (after reading or learning about the topic). TC explained how a KWL chart initially stumped her high school students:

> I know it seems simple, but if you saw these kids in the beginning of this year, just getting them to identify what they know about a topic was like pulling teeth. It was like, "Well what do you know about this? You know something about plants. One thing, please." So now I'm having them ask, "Okay, what more do I want to know about this?" Getting them to look beyond what's in front of them. And I would say that was the hardest part. And getting them to identify what they learned was the easy part, honestly.

Table 5.1. Examples of Lesson Objectives with Matching Assessments

	Lesson objectives	Assessment
Elementary example	**Content:** I can name community helpers. **Language:** I can speak and write my own sentences by using nouns and pronouns to identify community helpers with the support of sentence frames and pictures.	Erica assesses students' written sentences using a writing rubric. The rubric criteria and points for each are: • I used the correct vocabulary words. (2) • I used complete sentences. (2) • My writing makes sense. (2) • My writing is neat. (1) • I can read aloud my own sentences to the teacher. (1)
High School example	**Content:** Students will form a group and work together to assign roles, establish expectations, and make a plan. **Language:** Students will speak and listen to their group members to make a plan for the task.	Students fill out an exit ticket in Google Forms, which Melissa has posted in Google Classroom. The exit ticket questions are: 1. How did you collaborate or cooperate with your group today? What did you do? 2. Do you think that your group is ready to complete the task next week? 3. What can YOU do to make sure that your group is ready next week?

TC's example illustrates how students might have difficulty with the assessment task itself, in this case an unfamiliar KWL chart, not necessarily with the content—prior knowledge about plants. In addition to being unfamiliar with common types of assessment in general, multilingual students may also misunderstand directions given for completing an assessment. Unless you're careful to give clear instructions and confirm that students understand them, you may end up measuring a student's ability to understand your instructions rather than what their knowledge and skills are.

Another important factor in assessment design is authenticity, which refers to whether an assessment is meaningful to students and connected to real-world tasks. Authenticity also means the assessment should match instruction as closely as possible. For example, if you're teaching students how to write an essay, the assessment should be an essay rather than a multiple-choice quiz. That is, authentic assessment means that you assess students' performance with whatever students produce during an instructional activity—be it an essay, graphic organizer, poster, presentation, video, or demonstration. These are considered performance-based assessments, which give teachers "a variety of sources from which to obtain information about their ELL students and can provide a complete picture of what these students know, how they interpret the material, and what they are capable of doing" (DelliCarpini, 2009, p. 18).

Authentic assessments for multilingual students should include two important elements: visible criteria and self-assessment (Pierce, 2002). *Visible criteria* mean making it clear to students what is being assessed and how. *Self-assessments* give the students the space to reflect on their own performance. Both of these elements benefit multilingual students in particular, as they provide students with comprehensible input about the assessment, and further ways to show their understanding. A third important element is *feedback*, which students should receive from a variety of sources, including peers and instructors.

In the lessons that we observed, we saw many examples of teachers using informal assessments to support multilingual students:

- Chris took anecdotal notes of his 9th-grade students' partner dialogues as they jointly described a picture of the setting of a book.
- Kendall assessed her 3rd-grade students' written stories about their morning routines based on their completion of a graphic organizer. She expected students to describe four events with at least one complete sentence per event, using sequence words (first, then, next).
- Nancy circulated the room, giving written feedback on her high school students' projects, explaining what their scores meant and what they needed to do to get better, and having one-on-one conferences with students who had questions about their performance.
- Andrea had her 6th-grade students self-assess their sensory detail sentences using the WIDA language proficiency levels.
- TC assessed her students' oral presentations on plants based on a rubric with clear categories such as "organized," "loud and clear," and "understands material."

These assessments were humanizing because they were authentic measures of work students created during instruction; had clear expectations for students; included ways for students to assess and reflect on their performance; were comprehensible to students; and offered opportunities for success because the assessment was aligned with objectives and based on teachers' knowledge of what students could do with their existing resources. These ways of engaging in assessment are empowering because they center students in instruction, allow students to see progress, and offer students opportunities to demonstrate their content knowledge independent of language.

Interpreting Standardized Tests and Other Formal Assessments

Teachers' beliefs about the role of assessment are often mixed (Barnes et al., 2015): on one hand, teachers recognize the importance of assessment for student learning; on the other hand, teachers may view especially large-scale standardized tests as a "stick" meant to punish both them and their students, which may force teachers to spend inordinate amounts of time "teaching to the test." This is especially problematic for multilingual students, who are often subjected to a wider range of standardized tests than other students. As a result, multilingual students are at risk of losing even more valuable instructional time.

First, there are large-scale tests—usually at the state level—that measure students' progress toward grade-level standards in subjects such as ELA, math, and science. These tests are usually taken in the spring semester, involve multiple-choice, short-answer, and/or essay questions, and are now often conducted using computers. The test results of students who are designated "English learner" are tracked separately within the overall standardized test results. This is done to ensure states are fulfilling their obligation to provide students identified as ELs with quality education. However, it also means many of your multilingual students who still struggle with grade-level English may be subjected to tests they understand little about. Therefore, it is important for you to recognize that a state test score does not always accurately reflect a multilingual student's abilities and that it should only be used as one data point in any educational decisions about the student.

In addition to content-area tests, multilingual students may need to take a variety of English language proficiency tests. These are used to determine whether a student qualifies for, has made progress in, or is ready to exit English language development (ELD) services. Sometimes, the same test is used for all three purposes. The following are examples of widely used proficiency tests:

- WIDA ACCESS for ELLs, used in 41 states and territories
- Texas English Language Proficiency Assessment System (TELPAS)
- English Language Proficiency Assessments for California (ELPAC)
- Arizona English Language Learner Assessment (AZELLA)
- New York State Identification Test for English Language Learners (NYSITELL) and the New York State English as a Second Language Achievement Test (NYSESLAT)

These tests examine students' proficiency in English in all four language domains (listening, speaking, reading, and writing), and provide a score that indicates their proficiency in each domain, as well as an overall score indicating the student's proficiency level across domains. For example, on the WIDA ACCESS test, students can get a score between 1 and 6 in the different language domains as well as an overall score, which corresponds to different proficiency levels (entering, emerging, developing, expanding, bridging, and reaching).

Accurately interpreting data gleaned from English language proficiency tests is important for multilingual students because these interpretations have direct consequences at the individual student level, including decisions around whether a student needs to be enrolled in or exited from ELD services, as well as the level, intensity, and frequency of services delivered (Turkan & Buzik, 2016).

Finally, both mainstream teachers and ESOL specialists use a variety of standardized tests at the classroom or small-group level—including math and reading assessments, such as the Developmental Reading Assessment (DRA)— often given quarterly to help teachers monitor their students' progress with important skills and knowledge. Stephanie, an elementary ESOL teacher explained this:

> We had a staff meeting yesterday that looked at data from the state assessment and DRA scores in the school, so that got me thinking about how I'm building vocabulary knowledge with the students and whether I'm being rigorous enough with some of the 3rd-graders. They're not all actually ESOL-leveled at the same place, but their DRA level is similar, so I've grouped them so that I can see them at the same time when we're doing small groups. So I'm thinking about whether or not I'm really working in as much vocabulary as they can handle, because I think at the higher levels they can handle more at once with shorter explanations and practice.

As Stephanie's thoughts on her use of standardized test data illustrate, using information from such tests can then be used to group students, plan instruction, and set high expectations for student performance. Standardized classroom assessments can be used in humanizing ways, as Stephanie's comment illustrates, because she uses test results to challenge her own expectations about her students' ability to learn vocabulary.

Differentiating Assessments

Just as you would differentiate instruction for your students at different ability levels (see Chapter 3), it is important to differentiate your assessments with different types of modifications in order to more accurately gauge what students know and can do. Designing a differentiated assessment should begin with a consideration of the students' needs and strengths, which connects assessment to the core practice Knowing Students (see Chapter 1), since you need to know the students' linguistic readiness, cultural background, and prior knowledge to be able to differentiate the assessment in ways that are helpful to the student, yet maintain the integrity of the assessment. Melissa, a secondary ESOL ELA teacher, spoke of her experience:

> I had a history class for students new to the country and I learned students' needs. You just have to spend the time to make two or three different types of assessment because it's not fair for me to give them a failing grade on

this quiz that has questions they can't answer, like, "Which of the following is?" But the high-level learner, who's had formal schooling, they're ready for that. So my aim is that I *have* to make different assessments.

As Melissa's comment illustrates, it is time consuming but important to create different versions of an assessment to match your students' needs and strengths so that all students have the opportunity to show what they know and can be supported to grow academically. However, creating more than one version of an assessment may be needed, mainly with more traditional assessments such as quizzes. As Nancy noted, more authentic assessments create more favorable conditions for differentiation to take place naturally:

> When I taught using traditional assessments, what was really challenging was designing them for a population of students who are all over the place in their English proficiency and prior schooling. But I taught this past year through project-based learning. For example, I taught a unit on plot structure, and the assessment at the end was writing a narrative about students' own immigration experiences. It automatically differentiates the assessment for students because their narratives are going to be completely different, and they're going to be based on their experiences. So I found that assessing through projects really helped make it differentiated for students.

Thus, when possible, using authentic assessments allows you to differentiate more readily for students, and to more easily adjust your instruction to support their continued growth at different rates and with different support in place. As mentioned at the beginning of this chapter, differentiating assessments means adjusting the language-based expectations to the students' language proficiency level and providing appropriate supports and scaffolds for students who need them to be able to complete the assessment (Fairbairn & Jones-Vo, 2010). Differentiating an assessment can include:

- Giving a student fewer or more items to complete
- Giving a student fewer or more linguistic supports for completing the assessment, such as a word bank, sentence frames, a graphic organizer, a dictionary, or pictorial aids
- Giving a student a variety of assessments to choose from, such as a written report, cartoon, poster, or an oral presentation
- Giving a student more time in which to complete an assessment
- Offering a different environment in which the student can complete an assessment (for instance, in a separate space from the classroom)
- Providing different tools or a different format in which students can complete an assessment (for instance, with paper and pencil rather than typing on the computer; or providing an oral response rather than a written one)

Often, multilingual students who are entitled to ELD services are also entitled to accommodations on assessments. Some of the differentiation methods listed above are also used as official accommodations on summative and standardized assessments. However, accommodations differ from modifications for differentiating an assessment in that accommodations aren't supposed to markedly alter the assessment. For example, the student's accommodation plan might list "extended time, questions read aloud, and use of a word-to-word bilingual dictionary," which are accommodations that do not alter the content of the original assessment. It is important to help the student practice using their accommodations for everyday instruction and assessment before asking the student to use them during a high-stakes test.

Differentiation of assessment is humanizing because it allows students to display their individual strengths and gives accurate information for teachers to plan their supports for each student. Ideally, this differentiation process isn't separate from differentiation for instruction, but instead instruction and assessment—as well as differentiation—are planned through an integrated process.

SEEING IT IN ACTION

As discussed above, assessment is an important dimension of humanizing pedagogy, because without accurate and fair assessments, teachers and schools might make decisions that are harmful to multilingual students. It is particularly important for teachers of multilingual students to carefully consider what might be humanizing or dehumanizing about a particular assessment. This is because classroom assessments in U.S. schools are most often conducted using the English language, in which these students are often still developing proficiency. Furthermore, assessments frequently assume particular cultural knowledge, such as test questions that include references most familiar to students who have been raised in an environment with experiences typical for the White, middle-class, English-speaking culture.

The teachers we worked with understood the need to fairly and equitably assess their multilingual students' knowledge and skills. Below we highlight examples from Andrew and Melissa, who regularly employ humanizing assessments in their classrooms. Note how they design and use informal assessments to accurately and fairly gauge their students' performance, interpret assessments in order to inform their instruction, and differentiate assessments to match individual students' abilities.

Andrew

Andrew, an elementary ESOL teacher, is reading a book about the gingerbread man with a group of three 2nd-graders. His focus for the lesson is reading comprehension, with the emphasis on emotion words and idiomatic expressions. Notice how Andrew uses questioning, a form of informal assessment, to gauge his students' vocabulary knowledge and understanding of the story.

> After a brief introduction to some vocabulary that students would see in the picture book, Andrew asks his students to read the story aloud in a quiet voice, each at their own pace, while Andrew listens in, assessing students' reading and occasionally stopping to probe students' comprehension with questions. He stops David, one of the students, and asks him to make a prediction about the rest of the story.

> *David:* I think the fox is going to be a bad guy.
> *Andrew:* What makes you say that?
> *David:* He looks hungry.
> *Andrew:* So, he's hungry. What else makes you think he's going to be a bad guy?
> *David:* Because look at his face. And it says "sly." What does it mean?
> *Andrew:* What do you think it means?
> *David:* Hmm.
> *Andrew:* Well, if we're not sure about a word in the text, where can we look?
> *David:* The picture.
> *Andrew:* Try it. So, you said the text says, "He was a sly fox." So, let's look at the picture.
> *David:* I think he's going to lie to him.
> *Andrew:* Oh, he's going to lie. So he's pretty sneaky, right? He's tricky. So, that is exactly what sly means, if a person or a character is sly, they are sneaky or tricky.

> Once students are finished reading, Andrew gives feedback on their reading strategies, helping students understand how they were doing. During this conversation, David brings up the strategy he had used to figure out the meaning of the word "sly."

> *Andrew:* I want to say two things I really liked about your reading. The first one was this: I saw David constantly looking at the pictures. When he went to the page, he didn't just read fast, fast, fast, turn the page, read, read, read. He paused, he looked at the pictures, he read at a good rate, he made sure he was thinking about what he was reading. Jonathan did something similar. Jonathan, when he would finish a page, he would say what he thought: "Oh, I think the fox was a bad guy! Oh, they're having a hard time catching that

gingerbread man!" That tells me he was thinking about what he was reading, and that's what good readers do, so you guys used two strategies I really loved.

David: At first, I see the pictures.

Andrew: I noticed. And does it help you understand what the book is talking about?

David: Yeah, when I think that he was the bad fox, look at his eyes.

Next, Andrew uses a chart with emotion words and pictures of faces with different expressions to gauge students' understanding of the emotion the two main characters in the book were experiencing.

Andrew: Okay, we're going to talk about how the man and the woman feel, and we're going to use this to help us (pointing at the emotion word chart). When you look at their faces, and you think, "Oh, I know how they feel, but I don't know what word to use," you can use this to help you, so you can find a face that kind of looks like theirs.

Jonathan: And if you don't know what the word is to describe this face (points to the book), you can read this one (points to the chart).

Andrew: So, what about these two faces looks similar? (Points to the man in the book and the surprised face on the emotions chart.) You said these two look similar, and I agree, but what makes them look similar?

Jonathan: The mouth.

David: The eyes.

Andrew: What about the mouth? Oh, the eyes, too, David. What's happening with the mouth?

Jonathan: It's open.

Andrew: What about the eyes? Do his eyes look like they're closed, or do they look like they are big and open?

David: Big and open.

Andrew: I agree. So, okay, it looks like we agree that the old man is surprised. What do you think has made him surprised? Think for a second.

Jonathan: The woman is surprised too.

Andrew: So, tell us, David, what do you think has made the man surprised? Jonathan, I want you to listen, and then maybe you'll have something to add to it.

David: The gingerbread man come to life, and he run away.

Andrew: So, they were surprised because—

David: Because they see the gingerbread come to life.

Andrew writes, "The man and the woman are surprised because the gingerbread man came to life" on the whiteboard. Then, he directs students' attention to the phrase "come to life."

Andrew: The gingerbread man, we would say he *came* to life. Is that normal?

David: No.

Andrew: When your family makes cookies, do they come to life? Or, when you cook any type of food, does the food start talking and come to life?

David: No.

Andrew: No, so that—

David: It's surprising.

Andrew: That's pretty surprising.

David: They're going to catch him when he jumps.

Andrew: So, Jonathan, I want you to read this, and I want you to tell me if you agree and if there's anything you want to add (points at the sentence he wrote on the whiteboard).

Jonathan: The man and the woman were surprised because the gingerbread man came to life.

Andrew: Do you agree with that?

Jonathan: Yeah. And also, because when you cook food, the food doesn't come to life.

Andrew: Okay.

Jonathan: And when my mom cooks cookies, they don't move.

Andrew: So, let's add that sentence, and we can explain why that is surprising. (Starts writing the sentence and reads it aloud as he writes.) So, "They were surprised because . . ." what did you say?

Jonathan: Because cookies can't move.

Andrew: "Cookies can't . . ." What was the phrase we said? Not "move," but what did we say?

Jonathan: Cookies can't come to life.

Andrew: "Cookies can't come to life!" We're going to put an exclamation point because that really is surprising.

When we later discussed the lesson with Andrew, he noted how important it was for him to assess how well students understood difficult linguistic aspects of the story, such as idiomatic expressions, in addition to understanding the gist of the story.

I've been focusing more on idiomatic expressions and things like that—beyond just "Do you understand the story as a whole?"—and getting a little bit nitty gritty. Yesterday, we did a book about a baby bird that was in an egg, and she was running out of room in the egg. So we talked about the expression "running out of room," because my desk was a mess. So, I asked them, "Could you put this book on my desk?" and they were like, "Well, not really." I responded, "Yeah, because I ran out of room." And they were saying, "We were in the cafeteria, and there were all these trays, and we ran out of room"—they were using the phrases. And so in this book the idiomatic expression we were focusing on was the phrase "came to life."

We also discussed with Andrew the fact that he had continuously probed student thinking throughout the lesson by asking students questions such as, "Why do you say that?" "What makes you think that?" and "What evidence do you see in the pictures and the author's words?" Andrew noted that this type of formative assessment was a priority in his school:

> You know, that's actually been a big push this year, across the board at the school: "We want to see more accountable talk, like, Why do you think that? Do you agree? Do you disagree?"

By skillfully using questioning, Andrew was able to use informal assessment in ways that provided him with valuable information about the students' thought processes and comprehension of the story. While this was a priority for the whole school, Andrew's multilingual students benefited from this type of assessment because it allowed them to extend their thinking with each answer, gradually providing Andrew a more complete picture of their comprehension. Andrew also practiced humanizing assessment when he had students reflect on their own abilities as a form of self-assessment while he pointed out the comprehension strategies they had successfully used, and when he provided students with the emotion word chart as a visual aid to help them answer his comprehension questions about the book.

Melissa

Melissa's lesson for her secondary ESOL ELA class is a culminating activity in a poetry unit: students present their poetry circle discussions to Melissa while she circulates among small groups, assessing students with a rubric. Melissa had created what she called "level-ups" for her students, which were descriptions of five levels of increasing language complexity. She consistently used these descriptions to help her students see where their current English language proficiency level was and what they needed to do to rise to the next language proficiency level. Notice how Melissa uses this knowledge she gained from interpreting the formal language proficiency assessment to help students perform at the highest possible level:

> The class starts with students reading aloud the content and language objectives and "level-ups," which are posted on the board.

Melissa: I have some level-ups. This is what I'm looking for, so I want you to speak on your level, okay? Your level. So can somebody tell me, what is a Level 1?

Students read the different levels of language use posted on the board: (1) Words and phrases, (2) Simple sentences, (3) Some complex sentences, (4) Many complex and compound sentences, and (5) Extended conversation about the topic. Next, Melissa reminds students that she will grade their presentations using a rubric, which she had previously reviewed with them. She also asks students to be ready to discuss the poem based on their assigned group roles. One of these roles is "language analyzer"—a student in charge of discussing any special features in the poem, including capitalization, spacing, and repetition. Melissa approaches the first group and begins by assessing the student who has been assigned the role of language analyzer.

Melissa: So you do not need to write anything on this paper (holds up the rubric). This is just for me to grade you on your speaking. You need to focus on your group roles. Which poem did you choose?
Josefina: "Good Hot Dogs" (by Sandra Cisneros).
Melissa: Okay, I need my language analyzer. Katiana, can you tell me about the structure of the poem?
Katiana: A capital letter.
Melissa: So where did you find capitalization? Can you describe where it is?
Katiana: Primera palabra [First word].
Melissa: Okay, can you put that into English?
Katiana: The first letter.
Melissa: The first letter? And what is *palabra*?
Katiana: Word.
Melissa: Okay, the first word in the sentence. Did you see anything else?
Katiana: Two words are the same. Hot dogs.
Melissa: What is it called when two words are the same?
Katiana: Repetition.
Melissa: Okay and was there any special spacing? Spacing, you know spacing, are there any gaps in the lines?

(Katiana isn't sure how to answer.)

Melissa: It's okay, Katiana, it's okay. You're right on your speaking level. We'll practice until you feel more comfortable.

Next, Melissa assesses another student whose role is "summarizer."

Melissa: Can you tell me what the poem is about?
Leti: Hot dogs.
Melissa: What did they do with the hot dogs?
Leti: (No answer.)
Melissa: Did they smell the hot dogs?
Leti: No, eat.
Melissa: No, they ate them.

Melissa assesses each student similarly, making notes on her rubric as she speaks with each of them in turn.

As can be seen from the lesson vignette, some of Melissa's students were able to produce only single words or phrases as responses to her discussion questions about the poem. However, she prompted her students in different ways to elicit the highest-level answers they were able to produce. This gave her an opportunity to gauge students' speaking skills in more depth and differentiate her approach for each student.

After the lesson, Melissa explained the reason for her focus on assessing students' speaking skills, noting that her heterogeneous groups of students (based on English language proficiency) needed support in the form of different speaking opportunities. Adding more structure and scaffolding to speaking activities allowed her students to more fully participate in classroom conversations in different content areas. In addition, she described the importance of the assessment data for teachers in other content areas, who might need to know "where their kids actually are, what they need to do, and then teaching strategies for speaking to use in their own classroom." Melissa's comment illustrates an understanding of how assessments could support her own instruction but also that of other teachers, some of whom may not have been as familiar with multilingual students' language development. This type of collaboration with colleagues is discussed more in depth in Chapter 6.

Melissa also noted the importance of familiarizing the students with the assessment instruments, and the fact that this process would take time:

So schoolwide, we're doing speaking initiatives where we have a lot of rubrics now. I feel like later, when the kids are familiar with what it looks like and where they fall, and they are more familiar with our new language rubric, they'll be like, "Oh, I have to say things, like a lot of things, to move up to the next WIDA level."

Melissa's comment demonstrates that she was aware of the importance of teaching students to use tools such as rubrics to understand not only their current abilities but also what they would need to do to achieve the next level in their performance, so that they would eventually be able to exit ELD services altogether and be fully included in regular classroom instruction.

Melissa's lesson showed a scaffolded way of assessing students' speaking skills, where students were made aware of what was expected of them both at the next proficiency level they were striving to reach (the "level-ups" as Melissa called them) and in their group role (language analyzer, summarizer, etc.). Melissa's use of the rubric to measure students' performance was an authentic way of assessing the actual product of the poetry circles—the discussion—and allowed her to see whether each student was successful both in their role and at their level. The assessment allowed her to differentiate her expectations for students at different proficiency levels. Melissa also demonstrated the ability to interpret and utilize standardized assessment data to create the rubric based on her students' levels from the WIDA ACCESS test. The result was a differentiated assessment that produced meaningful evidence of speaking performance both for her and for her students. This was humanizing because it offered students an authentic opportunity to showcase their skills.

TAKE ACTION IN YOUR CLASSROOM

- Develop your assessment literacy by analyzing the assessments you're using in class. Do they measure content, language, or both? Make sure you know what you're measuring. If the assessment is focused on content, think about what language supports students may need to demonstrate their content knowledge separately from their language skills. If the assessment is focused on language, make sure students are familiar with the content so that a lack of content knowledge doesn't interfere with their production.
- Make sure you're using clear instructions so that the assessment is measuring what students know about a topic, and they are able to engage with the task at hand.
- Evaluate the need to make your assessments more authentic. Instead of quizzes or short-answer exit tickets at the end of a lesson, consider whether the instructional activities completed during the lesson will yield a product you can assess.
- Check your students' standardized test scores, both in state content standard tests and their English proficiency tests. If you don't have these, find out how to get them. Then, think about how the results can inform your instruction. Consult another expert in your school if needed—for example, a content-area lead teacher, a reading or math specialist, or an ESOL specialist.
- When planning a lesson and designing differentiated approaches for instructing your students, also think about ways you can differentiate your assessment. For example, choose one assessment at the medium level most of your students will be able to complete, and then design

an assessment for one level up and one level down, with fewer or more language supports.

QUESTIONS FOR REFLECTION

1. Think about the assessments you use in the classroom. Do they have humanizing aspects? That is, are they giving both you and your students accurate information about their content and language skills? Are they authentic? Do they contain opportunities for student self-assessment? If the answer is no to any of these, what can you do to change them?
2. Reflect on your assessment literacy regarding the standardized assessments your students take. What do you know about the assessments and how their results should be interpreted and used? Do you see ways the results might be biased against your multilingual students, and if so, what could you do to advocate for a better approach to their interpretation?
3. Why is differentiating assessments just as necessary as differentiating instruction for your multilingual students? How can differentiating provide you with more accurate assessment information about your students?

CHAPTER 6

Relationships and Advocacy

> I learned how important a supportive and collaborative work environment
> is for young teachers. Some people are able to go it alone, taking on the
> multitude of daily challenges without the help of supportive colleagues, but
> most young teachers don't work that way. We need modeling, ideas, and
> guidance. We need a sense that others are invested in the same fight and that
> there are people that know what they're doing.
>
> —Chris, secondary ESOL teacher

Building relationships of dignity, care, and respect is at the center of humanizing pedagogies, and these relationships are a core component of engaging in advocacy to support multilingual students, families, and communities. Chris's comment above reminds us that new teachers need additional support, guidance, and opportunities to collaborate with colleagues in order to best support learners. Teaching all students, but multilingual students in particular, is a collaborative endeavor that includes multiple stakeholders. Students, teachers, administrators, families, and communities are expected to work together to best support the range of academic, linguistic, and social-emotional learning abilities and needs of multilingual students.

Strong relationships among these stakeholders are necessary so that multilingual students and their teachers are surrounded by an informed and committed community of support that will promote equitable policies and everyday instructional practices (Martin-Beltrán & Peercy, 2012; Peercy & Martin-Beltrán, 2011). These relationships are also critical in order to bring awareness to the unique needs and challenges of multilingual students, their families, and communities, and to advocate for students to have access to resources that will allow them to flourish in and out of school (Hamayan & Field, 2012; Milner et al., 2018).

Working with multilingual students and their families is a rewarding experience for most teachers. However, there are a number of additional demands for teachers who work with multilingual students. To cope with the additional demands and stress of the profession, teachers of multilingual students must take time to regularly engage in self-care (Peercy et al., 2019a). Practicing self-care consistently has potential to reduce daily stress, enhance mental and physical well-being, and promote a more positive learning environment for teachers and multilingual students (Jennings, 2015).

DIMENSIONS OF ENGAGING IN RELATIONSHIP-BUILDING AND ADVOCACY

In this chapter, we will discuss dimensions of this core practice that teachers can enact to develop positive relationships with different stakeholders in order to support multilingual students, and to advance advocacy efforts. Specifically, we will explore the following:

- Collaborating with colleagues
- Making meaningful connections with families
- Engaging in advocacy with a variety of stakeholders (including administrators, policymakers, and the community)
- Practicing teacher self-care in a particularly demanding field in education

Taking up this core practice requires that teachers be intentional and deliberate in developing and sustaining important, meaningful, and delicate relationships with colleagues, families, and community partners. These relationships are at the heart of teaching, learning, and advocacy. It is essential that you are equipped to professionally communicate and work with different people in your students' lives to ensure that your multilingual students are appropriately supported in classrooms, schools, and communities, and through policies that impact their education. Engaging in relationship-building and advocacy is complex, challenging, and necessary work, and regularly engaging in self-care to help you manage the daily demands and stress of the profession is critical.

Relationships do not happen by chance; rather, relationships happen by choice. This requires that you carefully consider how you will develop positive relationships with your multilingual students by getting to know them (see Chapter 1) and promoting a positive learning environment (see Chapter 2). Teachers should also consider how they will build and sustain positive relationships with colleagues and the families of their multilingual students. Meaningful relationships are important because they "give us a sense of belonging in the group, a sense of identity in contrast to others in that group, an almost therapeutic support system, and a reason not to feel lonely, isolated or disconnected from social dynamics" (Howard, 2017, p. 6).

Networks of strong relationships are particularly important for multilingual students so that teachers can gain a deeper understanding of the student's cultural background, strengths, and needs in and out of school by connecting with families, community members, and other teachers who know the various facets of your students and their contexts well. Relationship-building, however, is a process that takes time to develop. Person-centered behaviors that demonstrate care, empathy, responsiveness, and warmth can help build positive relationships with colleagues, families, and even yourself (Cornelius-White, 2007). Below, we will consider ways for teachers to collaborate with colleagues, make meaningful connections with families, engage in advocacy with a variety of stakeholders, and practice self-care.

Collaborating with Colleagues

Teachers who specialize in teaching multilingual students work with many different colleagues: mainstream classroom teachers (e.g., math, science, social studies, English, PE technology, music, art) as well as other ESOL teachers, special education teachers, counselors, administrators, instructional coaches, and school personnel. Research has demonstrated that collaborating with colleagues can greatly improve classroom instruction and ultimately benefit multilingual students' learning experiences (DelliCarpini, 2008).

Erica, an elementary ESOL teacher, explained that a strong focus on building positive relationships with colleagues can cultivate a pathway for much needed collaboration:

> Teaching how to teach ESOL to content teachers has been a bigger and bigger part of our work as ESOL specialists. I'm starting to realize that if I don't start to do a better job of doing that, then I'm not serving my students well, so I need to build relationships. A part of that is building a positive relationship with and collaborating with mainstream classroom teachers, but also figuring out how to show mainstream teachers another way to scaffold, or point out to them what might be difficult about this particular math assessment linguistically.

Peercy and Martin-Beltrán (2011) note the multiple benefits when ESOL teachers and their grade-level colleagues come together, stating that these collaborative efforts can offer "a broader network of resources for ELLs by bringing together more people, materials, ideas, and abilities" than what can be accomplished independently, with a larger goal of making language and content more accessible for multilingual students (p. 659).

There are several ways for ESOL teachers and mainstream colleagues to engage in collaborations that have potential to benefit multilingual students. See Table 6.1 for some common ways to engage with colleagues.

These models ask ESOL and mainstream educators to participate in meaningful conversations and critical reflections about issues related to lesson planning, instructional practices, or analyzing multilingual students' work (Peercy & Martin-Beltrán, 2011). Peercy and Martin-Beltrán (2011) found that "when ESOL and mainstream teachers spend time together in the mainstream classroom, the ESOL teacher has access to the kinds of demands 'on the ground' that the mainstream classroom generates for ELLs, and an

Table 6.1. Collaborating with Colleagues

Collaboration Type	Description
Co-Planning	Co-planning is when colleagues jointly plan lessons together to ensure that different aspects (e.g., language and content) of a lesson are covered.
Co-Teaching	There are many types of co-teaching models. Examples of some common forms include teachers taking turns leading the class, working with rotations of small groups, or one teacher teaching the whole class while the other teacher assists individual learners.
Observing Colleagues to Provide Feedback	Observing colleagues occurs when a teacher carefully watches a colleague actively working with learners. Professional discussions about the observation usually occur afterward, providing constructive feedback and sharing ideas about what was observed.
Critical Friends Group	Critical Friends Groups (CFGs) bring together a group of colleagues (and often an instructional coach) to improve classroom practices. Individual members of the CFGs identify goals for their students and classrooms, brainstorm strategies for reaching the identified goals, and collect data to determine progress and further modifications.
Professional Learning Communities	In many school districts, Professional Learning Communities (PLCs) bring together educators to meet regularly, collaboratively explore topics of interest they have identified, and share expertise.

opportunity to share context-specific feedback with the mainstream teacher about the challenges that ELLs experience and resources they bring to that setting" (p. 670).

For instance, Andrew, an elementary ESOL teacher, discussed how he worked with his 1st-grade colleague both in and out of the classroom to improve his instruction for his learners:

> This year we have participated in a peer collaboration initiative, so I've been doing a cycle with a peer where I'll come to see her guided reading and we will debrief. Then, we will co-plan a lesson together and then we will observe each other's lesson that we co-planned. It's been really cool because the other person will point out things that maybe you didn't see the first time.

Here are some tips for co-planning lessons:

- Establish a positive relationship with your colleague. This will serve as a strong foundation for any collaborative efforts.

- Respect the knowledge and expertise each person can contribute to planning for instruction.
- Create a schedule for planning together. Honor the schedule and time to connect.
- Use technology such as electronically shared folders, documents, and other online resources to collaborate and share information about students quickly and more efficiently.
- Share a common lesson template and/or tools that expedite and support planning.
- Have open dialogues about lesson goals, accomplishments, and areas for refinement.
- Keep the focus on the students: How can co-planning with colleagues benefit multilingual students?

Melissa, a secondary ESOL ELA teacher, explained that collaborating with colleagues was built into the culture of her high school—and expected of the faculty. She shared some ways that she and her colleagues come together each week to plan lessons, observe, and reflect upon their efforts:

> The music, technology, PE, and ESOL teachers decided that we would teach students the same collaborative practices as well as utilize the same vocabulary to give students exposure in different content areas to reinforce their learning. We are observing each other's class and planning weekly in this effort.

Not only can collaboration with colleagues enhance instruction for multilingual students, but engaging in positive collaborations with colleagues can offer benefits for ESOL and mainstream educators, too. Dove and Honigsfeld (2010) highlight the following benefits of teachers working with each other:

- Reduction in feelings/experiences of isolation
- More opportunities to share expertise with other colleagues
- Higher potential for quality ESOL programs

Dove and Honigsfeld (2010) also observed that ESOL and mainstream teachers who demonstrate a commitment to promoting social justice and humanizing pedagogies actively seek opportunities to collaborate with their colleagues, as this has potential to disrupt inequities and strengthen instruction for multilingual learners. Indeed, ESOL and mainstream teachers must engage in meaningful, collaborative work to best support multilingual students. You should also carefully consider how other school personnel—including administrators, instructional assistants, classroom tutors, hallway/playground monitors, guidance counselors, administrative assistants/secretaries, nurses, custodians, bus drivers, and cafeteria workers—are trained to create and support a positive learning environment for multilingual learners (Crandall et al., 2012).

Making Meaningful Connections with Families

Multilingual students, families, and teachers all take part in interactions that have consequences for teaching, learning, and academic achievement. When teachers build positive relationships with the families of their multilingual students, they can better understand who multilingual students are and the cultural and linguistic resources and needs of the learners and their families. Research demonstrates that building strong relationships with families can lead to positive academic outcomes for multilingual students in schools (Auerbach, 2012). Such benefits can include less disruptive behaviors, better attendance, and higher graduation rates (Milner et al., 2018).

We use the term "family" to identify people who are involved in multilingual learners' lives in and out of school. We recognize that families can include a range of people who offer different kinds of care and support to multilingual students (Ishimaru, 2020). It is important to understand and respect that family structures will vary among students. For example, multilingual students might live with birth parents, grandparents, aunts, uncles, or cousins; friends who are like family; or state-appointed guardians. They might come from homes where more than one language is used or where English is never used. This can impact how you approach building and sustaining positive relationships with your students' families.

It is also important to approach relationship-building with families from an asset-based perspective. From this perspective, we acknowledge that families hold "the greatest expertise on their own children, their learning priorities and needs, their languages and cultural practices, their histories and nondominant ways of knowing" and as educators, we must work *with* families to *co-construct* culturally and linguistically responsive and sustaining pedagogies (Ishimaru, 2020, p. 13).

Milner and colleagues (2018) also encourage teachers to engage in partnerships with families that are "meaningful and collaborative relationships that benefit everyone involved" (p. 120). Asset-based perspectives focus on the strengths that families bring to the school partnership and recognize the many ways that families are involved in their multilingual students' schooling experiences. Consider the families who work—sometimes at multiple jobs—to ensure their learners have food, shelter, and clean clothing; or the families who might not be able to help with homework due to language barriers or lack of knowledge of the topic, but who consistently provide moral support, encouragement, and love that motivates their learners to participate in school. These are all meaningful ways that families contribute to student learning.

Additional ways of partnering with families who feel comfortable and are able to come to the school might include family representation in school governance, serving as paid assistants (i.e., school monitors, tutors, translators), or working as community liaisons or advocates (Meyers & Rodriguez, 2012). The larger goal of these types of partnerships is to create a "team of allied adults all trying to help students succeed in school" (Thompson, 2018, p. 161).

This perspective runs counter to deficit-based models of parental involvement that situate multilingual students and their families as less capable, less prepared, less educated, and less competent than English-dominant peers and families in school settings. Such models solely focus on limited activities that are strictly defined and controlled *by* schools—like helping with homework, volunteering in classrooms, chaperoning field trips, attending open houses or parent teacher conferences, serving on the Parent Teacher Association (PTA), or participating in fundraising efforts.

Families of multilingual students who do not consistently participate in these school-centered practices are often judged as "uncaring," "uninvolved," or "uninterested"—yet the reasons why some families might be reluctant or unable to participate are valid. For example, some families might not be able to attend these events due to work constraints or lack of childcare, while others might not feel welcome or comfortable at the school, especially if they are unfamiliar with the policies and practices of the school, or if there are no bilingual teachers or interpreters available. Some families might not be aware of the expectation that families engage with the school to support their learner in U.S. schools. They might deliberately stay away or not ask questions to demonstrate respect for teachers because they view teachers as the experts in their profession.

Communication with the families of multilingual students is essential to creating a bridge between families and schools and to better understand your families' needs. When teachers do not share a common language (or culture) with the families of their students, sometimes clear and consistent communication can be challenging. Erica grappled with this issue, and decided to make it a priority:

> My goal is going to be connecting with parents and families, especially because I don't speak Spanish. I want to get better at finding ways to communicate with parents and families. It's easy for me to feel afraid of doing that because I don't speak their language, but then what do I expect them to do? I need to be more courageous about calling and not be afraid to make phone calls and have parents come in to meet with me.

It is crucial that you set up systems to establish and maintain communication across the year. Establishing communication with families can be accomplished by calling the home; sending an email or physical letter, postcard, or flier; or hosting an in-person or virtual open house/orientation. After you have made initial contact with families of your multilingual students, it is important that you maintain such communications. Here are a few ideas to sustain conversations across the year:

- Set up a classroom website or social media outlet, which you frequently update

- Send weekly emails to provide class news and updates
- Make phones calls to the home for extended conversation
- Create YouTube videos that contain important information (note that closed captioning in different languages can be utilized)
- Utilize mobile apps that can translate messages into different languages
- Provide notebooks or folders to allow for daily communication between you and your families
- Survey multilingual students and their families frequently to ensure that you are inviting open communication

You should also consider reaching out to families to share good news or highlights about their learners rather than only focus on the challenges you encounter. This demonstrates a level of care and tells the family that you are committed to working with them to maintain a positive learning environment. If you meet in-person with the family, pay careful attention to their extralinguistic cues and respond appropriately, ensuring that your own body language appears professional and welcoming. In addition, if you are using an interpreter to facilitate the meeting, make sure that the interpreter knows how to accurately translate school jargon to families (many school districts employ interpreters who are specifically trained for this), and that even with an interpreter present, you are directing your words and eye contact at the family members. Families are critical partners in education, as they hold a deep knowledge and understanding of their learners. Making connections with families is vital and also helps humanize your teaching because you can learn more about the needs and assets of your students and families and use this information to strengthen academic and social-emotional learning in the classroom.

Engaging in Advocacy

Multilingual students and their families are often marginalized by educational policies and practices that do not fully meet their unique cultural, linguistic, social-emotional, and academic needs. Often, they are not well positioned to question, resist, or even recommend more appropriate alternatives to such ineffective policies and practices (Wright, 2015). ESOL educators also find themselves grappling with challenges of the profession that impact their ability to effectively and appropriately serve their learners (e.g., limited curriculum, materials, and resources) and their families (e.g., lack of clear and consistent communication). For these reasons and many more, teachers need to become familiar with ways to engage in advocacy in order to effectively and appropriately serve as an advocate for multilingual students, their families, and even the profession.

Dubetz and de Jong (2011) describe advocacy as going beyond the daily expectations of serving students in classrooms and acting on the behalf of others. We consider advocacy a key practice for working with multilingual students, their families, and the profession because of the potential to disrupt inequities in educational policies and deficit-oriented instructional practices that manifest in schools and classrooms and potentially disenfranchise entire communities. Consider the situations presented in Table 6.2 that teachers of multilingual students often encounter, and some of the possible responses that advocate for students. These are all issues that require advocacy to ensure that equitable practices are implemented.

At times, teachers will serve as advocates on behalf of multilingual students and their families with colleagues and administrators at the school. For

Table 6.2. Advocacy Responses to a Variety of Situations

Challenge	Possible advocacy response
You do not have your own classroom to teach multilingual students; instead you are assigned to teach in a hallway, closet, or nurse's office.	Lobby for better learning environments by discussing the cognitive demands that multilingual students encounter when learning content and language together. Also discuss how a poor learning environment can impact both academic achievement and self-esteem.
A mainstream colleague is not offering learning opportunities that build on the multilingual student's language or knowledge.	To center the needs of the student, engage in a professional conversation with your colleague about instructional practices that are developmentally appropriate and match the student's English language proficiency levels and content knowledge.
Your multilingual student is very frustrated because they have been placed in wrong course sections multiple times due to errors in reporting and interpreting their English language proficiency test scores.	Meet with mainstream colleagues, school counselors, administrators, and instructional coaches to reconcile the issue. Learn how to interpret language proficiency test scores and request support if the test scores are not an appropriate reflection of the student's linguistic abilities in English. Follow up with the different stakeholders until the issue is resolved.
You teach in a community where ICE has raided local apartment buildings, places of employment, and school grounds, looking for undocumented immigrant adults. Your multilingual students are terrified to come to school for fear that they or a loved one will be deported.	Have current, reliable information about the rights of undocumented immigrants, as well as resources to share if a loved one is under the threat of deportation.

example, Stephanie, an elementary ESOL teacher, described an instance when she needed to speak to a mainstream colleague about the instruction one of her ESOL students was receiving in the mainstream classroom when her colleague was asking the student to simply trace letters. Stephanie was able to talk with her colleague and explain that the student was capable of engaging in more cognitively and linguistically demanding tasks and successfully advocated for more complex learning opportunities for the student.

Other times, you might find yourself advocating for your learners by working with lawyers, politicians, policymakers, council members, and/or educational consultants on educational policies or even litigation surrounding issues like language policies, school conditions, curriculum/textbook adoptions, or transportation (Roos, 2020). Melissa discussed working with colleagues to advocate for resource allocation for new schools being built within her district: "We've been fighting and advocating for our school. I was at the county council meeting until 10:30pm . . . they need to fully fund the budget. This is about our building!"

Kendall, an elementary ESOL teacher, also reminded our team about the importance of knowing current policy information and contacting local government representatives on issues related to undocumented multilingual students and their families in order to engage in advocacy efforts:

> The ICE [Immigration and Customs Enforcement] raids are a really good reason to contact your representative . . . school teachers who are concerned about the kids and because people don't know what the policies are, there's a lot of fear of the unknown, even among the teachers. Just contacting your representative is a really good way to voice that to someone who will hopefully be able to make a difference.

Hamayan and Field (2012) highlight two critical issues when engaging in advocacy on behalf of multilingual students and their families: (1) We must advocate equitably and be mindful that multilingual students should not be treated as "the same" as other students because their needs are different from other students; and (2) a larger goal of advocacy is empowerment so that multilingual students, families, and their communities can become activists and take up this work on their own behalf. This means that you recognize your multilingual students and their families as cultural beings, each with unique backgrounds and life experiences that need to be acknowledged, understood, and supported appropriately. In order to be a "true agent of change," Santiago-Negrón (2012) states that "you must create situations that allow the community to speak together loudly and allow the community to be understood regardless of the language spoken" (p. 239).

There are also many other ways for teachers to engage in advocacy. Consider the opportunity to provide professional development to colleagues on topics that support linguistic, academic, and social-emotional learning and development for multilingual students and their families; or consider how you can encourage colleagues and administrators to adopt instructional programs and practices that are research-based and center on advancing multilingual students' languages, literacies, and content-area knowledge. Some teachers might seek to co-plan (and co-teach) with colleagues who serve multilingual students to ensure students' academic and language learning needs are being met. Minimally, all teachers can gather community-based resources for in-the-moment requests or have points of contact for additional support for multilingual students and their families within the larger community.

Wright (2012, 2015) also recommends the following actions that teachers can take to support multilingual students and their families:

- Accommodate families' language needs so they have current, credible information (in verbal and written form) in their home languages
- Understand federal and state policies for multilingual students and use the positive aspects of the policies to support learners
- Keep data to show the progress of multilingual students in learning languages and academic content
- Work to create change to current policies that are potentially harmful to your multilingual students and their families (e.g., talk with colleagues, administrators, families, community members about the ways in which the policy is harmful)
- Serve and encourage parents to serve on key school, district, and state committees
- Join professional organizations and networks
- Read professional literature on advocacy and advocacy issues;
- Connect with other educators, policymakers, and stakeholders through professional websites, listservs, blogs, and Twitter feeds
- Increase opportunities for family collaboration in your school
- Host family literacy programs
- Hold parent and family night events throughout the school year
- Take or send parents to local and national conferences

Advocacy has the potential to promote social justice and humanize pedagogy by centering the assets and needs of multilingual students and their families. As an educator, you play a very important role as a potential agent of change who can inform educational policy issues and everyday practices that positively impact multilingual students, their families, and the profession. Santiago-Negrón (2012) reminds us that advocacy is also about supporting these stakeholders as they advocate for themselves, too. Finally, advocacy is also about developing the positive relationships highlighted in this chapter as well as other community partnerships. These relationships are critical and must be nurtured and supported across time.

Practicing Self-Care

Teaching is a demanding and stressful profession that requires engaging in mindfulness and practicing self-care. Self-care is described as tending to your mind and thoughts, physical body, spiritual health, emotions, and your overall well-being. For teachers, self-care should take place both at home and at school. For example, at home you might incorporate regular exercise, or set clear boundaries between school life and work life to ensure that you are able to enjoy personal time away from the demands of the profession. While at school, you might also practice deep-breathing techniques, take brain breaks for yourself, and ensure that you are eating well to be fueled for the day. Teachers who regularly engage in self-care can lessen accumulated stress in their daily lives and this can support better relationships with students, colleagues, and families, which will result in a more positive learning environment for everyone (Jennings, 2015; Jennings et al., 2013).

Practicing self-care is critical, especially for ESOL teachers of multilingual students, as they often face additional stressors within the profession. Feeling devalued within the profession, receiving limited support from mainstream colleagues who might not understand the work of ESOL teachers, having a lack of control over the teaching environment, and processing the secondary trauma from multilingual students who have experienced trauma are a few of the common stressors identified by novice ESOL teachers (Peercy et al., 2019a).

The teachers we worked with all shared instances of feeling stressed and overwhelmed by the profession, especially in their first years of teaching, and often expressed a need for better self-care. For example, Andrea reflected on her ability to engage in this important work:

> For me, practicing self-care this year has come and gone in waves. I have found ways to either meet my needs, or to cope with life when those needs aren't being met; but I have not yet found a sustainable rhythm, and only time will tell how the fallout from my lack of self-care is affecting and will affect my family, friends, coworkers, and students. . . . I remain extremely determined to find a sustainable rhythm where my personal needs are met on a consistent basis so that I can give my best to the students and to the profession.

As Andrea describes, regularly engaging in self-care is an ongoing process, but the benefits are immense and can help you cope with the many sources of stress you grapple with in school and at home. Such benefits can include the following:

- A more balanced emotional state of well-being
- Increased compassion, empathy, and understanding of others
- Better focus and concentration
- An increased understanding of yourself

Each person must find their own "rhythm" or way to practice self-care, but this work is *necessary* in order to remain in the profession.

Practicing self-care can also contribute to a sense of community and belonging because you are actively seeking to engage in positive, supportive relationships with yourself and your colleagues—a key component in teaching multilingual students. For instance, Kendall made a strong connection between the importance of self-care, and positive relationships and effective collaboration between colleagues. She noted, "Without getting classroom teacher buy-in, feeling supported by your team, and taking care of yourself, I think it would be difficult to be an effective teacher and not burn out."

Practicing self-care can help you to improve your teaching because your personal needs are met, and you are better prepared to meet your personal and professional challenges in healthier and more productive ways—and greatly reduce the chance of teacher burnout. You are also much better able to engage in humanizing relationships with your students when you are in humanizing relationships yourself.

SEEING IT IN ACTION

This chapter highlights the importance of collaborating with colleagues, making meaningful connections with families, engaging in advocacy, and practicing self-care. These dimensions of the core practice are also central to humanizing pedagogy for multilingual students because the needs of the learners, their families, and their teachers who support them are respected and promoted. A strong focus on building positive relationships with different stakeholders can help to create informed communities of care, support, and action.

Here we share examples from Andrea, Melissa, and Erica as they discuss the importance of building and sustaining positive relationships with colleagues and engaging in advocacy.

Andrea

Andrea, an elementary ESOL teacher, reflects on how she engages in relationship-building and collaborating with two of her mainstream colleagues from math and ELA:

> The classroom teacher in math is the most flexible in terms of letting me come into the classroom and do things in the moment, but also pull the students out to do lessons. The math teacher and I realized that he struggles with how to write clear word problems for students. I think my giving the students that extra support in math has been a good focus area. At first, it was a little rough—the math teacher wondered "Why are you changing your schedule? Why are you pulling my students now?" but I think he's starting to understand that it is helping.

In this example, Andrea was able to provide additional support for students struggling with word problems in math class because she had a positive, collaborative relationship with the math teacher that allowed her to work with the students in a flexible way. She also shared how she collaborated with the 6th-grade ELA teacher:

> I've been co-teaching with the English language arts teacher, and I've been able to do some whole-group lessons, some mini-lessons on language points, and then also work with the students in the classroom more than pulling them out into small group settings. . . . There have been good parts, and there have been bad parts. I've been building my relationship with her, and we've been talking about next year and what we want it to look like. We're testing things out and seeing what we want to plan for the upcoming year, so that's exciting too!

Andrea's comments highlight some of the challenges and the affordances when sharing multilingual students in different types of ESOL contexts (i.e., pull-out, plug-in, and co-teaching models) with different teachers. The logistics of scheduling times to meet with students and colleagues can be complicated, but with clear and consistent communication and maintaining a positive and respectful working relationship with colleagues, multilingual students can benefit from the teachers' collaboration. Having strong collaborative working relationships with colleagues can help to create more humanizing and equitable learning opportunities for multilingual students because mainstream and ESOL teachers can work together to ensure they are providing academic rigor in their instruction, and multilingual students' linguistic resources in their home language and English are being fully utilized.

Melissa

During one of our team meetings, Melissa, a secondary ESOL ELA teacher, shared about a situation involving advocacy that took place during her internship in an elementary classroom with a 4th-grade teacher:

> I had a teacher make a really inappropriate comment about an Indian ESOL student—it was a racist comment about how she smelled like curry. It was her homeroom teacher, and it just kind of came out of nowhere. I was very stunned in the moment. It took me a moment to realize what she said. After talking with her, I thought, "What do I do?" and I thought, "I have to do something, like stand up for my student," because this was not appropriate.

Melissa's reflection highlights serious issues that can take place in schools that have lasting, harmful consequences for multilingual students. Even as a new student teacher, Melissa recognized the potential of such comments to harm this student (and others) and she decided to engage in a form of advocacy to challenge the racist comments made by the 4th-grade teacher, with the guidance and support of additional colleagues:

> With the help of my mentor teacher and the guidance counselor, we determined that it warranted a discussion with the teacher. My mentor teacher and the guidance counselor gave me the option of having the conversation with the teacher myself or letting my mentor teacher address the situation with her. I was really nervous. I didn't want to start a conflict. The teachers happened to be in the 4th-grade team meeting, so all the 4th-grade teachers were there. I was really nervous and it was really stressful, but it was good to go in and have this conversation with her and explain that what she said was really racist.

Though Melissa felt uncomfortable with this situation given her role as a student teacher, she sought guidance from a mentor teacher and the school guidance counselor to determine the best course of action. While it was not clear if the student heard the teacher's racist comments, Melissa served as an advocate and an ally to the multilingual student by having a conversation with the 4th-grade team about the language that was used regarding the student's scent, and how this was harmful and racist. This also reflected humanizing pedagogy because Melissa sought to create a positive learning environment for students where culture and relationships that promote dignity and care with students were valued.

Erica

Erica, an elementary ESOL teacher, reflects on her first year of teaching, with a focus on some of the lessons she learned about the stressors of the profession, but especially the need for self-care:

> One thing that I learned this year—that sounds so obvious, but I learned it the hard way—was that I need to take care of myself. I feel like I see teachers burn out. It's just something that I feel like the profession, as a whole, needs to talk about more in relation to being a teacher, and continuing to be a good teacher. I felt like in my first year, I was so overwhelmed with "Are you meeting the standards?" and, you know, "Where's your data?" and, "If you don't have the right data, why don't you have the right data?" All of these ways of trying to measure things, and I think I got lost in that. I think probably my instruction suffered from that for a little while until I was able to, kind of, get back on track.

Erica's comments reflect some of the additional stressors associated with the profession that are not often discussed in teacher preparation programs, including the pressure of collecting and managing data to demonstrate multilingual students' growth. This work is *in addition to* daily planning and instruction and involves summarizing and synthesizing data points, which can have consequences for both multilingual students and teachers. For Erica, this process was stressful and prompted her to recognize the need to engage in self-care so that she did not burn out. She also offered some advice:

> If I could go back and give myself advice during that first year, it would be to find the people in the school who you feel kind of a kinship with outside of work . . . finding other teachers who were really empathetic and understanding and could listen and give feedback when you need it. Find those people in the building as soon as you can and lean on them because everyone goes through it, and I feel like everyone understands it.

Engaging in self-care is considered a dimension of humanizing pedagogy because teachers like Erica must be able to manage the daily stress of the profession in order to support multilingual students in and out of school, and also teach learners how to engage in self-care as well. Colleagues can offer the kinds of support you might need because they understand what you are going through and can likely offer help and advice.

TAKE ACTION IN YOUR CLASSROOM

- Building positive relationships and getting to know your fellow educators can enhance opportunities for collaborating with colleagues to best support your multilingual students. Understand your various roles in relation to working with and supporting multilingual students. Work to engage in reciprocal relationships where you learn from your colleagues and your colleagues learn from you. Offer professional development sessions that focus on the unique language, learning, and social-emotional learning needs of the multilingual students that you serve. Maintain communication throughout the year.
- Families are a positive factor in students' academic and social growth, so it is critical that you make meaningful connections with families of your multilingual students. Welcome them into your school by offering school tours and orientations, having appropriate resources available, and creating an inclusive environment. Be sure to establish communication with your families right away and maintain communication as frequently, and consistently, as possible through multiple forms (e.g., fliers, email, class websites, or other types of communication apps). This also means that you offer oral and written support in the families' languages (e.g., you can enlist help from an interpreter or translation app), you engage in active listening and are responsive to families' needs and requests, and you are always respectful when talking about their learners.

- Engaging in advocacy means that you are informed about the legal mandates, policies, and the basic rights of multilingual students that you serve. Be sure to maintain positive, reciprocal relationships with different stakeholders who make decisions on the educational opportunities for multilingual students and their families. Become a consumer of the research surrounding the assets and needs of multilingual students and ensure that you are using practices in your classroom to humanize pedagogy and support their academic, linguistic, and social-emotional learning. Engage with your multilingual students and their families so that they can advocate for themselves, and support them in their advocacy efforts.
- Practicing self-care and self-compassion can support mindfulness and, in turn, help you manage stress associated with the profession and prevent you from feeling depleted and burned out. Try establishing a consistent work schedule to become more organized and maintain a routine, as this can help you in these endeavors. That means you will need to prioritize your daily duties and even set time limits on tasks. This can help you to establish clear boundaries between work and home. At school, take time to engage in "little things" throughout the day that bring you joy or give you a moment to separate yourself from the stress of the profession: Go for a walk down the hall or around the school, have a small treat during the day and savor it (e.g., food, drink, or something that brings you joy), or do a 3-minute meditation to engage in silence and reflection. Continue with additional self-care practices outside school (e.g., mindful eating, daily exercise, appropriate sleep, positive connections with friends and family) to sustain a healthier, more balanced life. Remember, you are a model for your multilingual students, so creating space to talk about and practice self-care with your learners and how these practices manifest in their lives can also support their social-emotional learning development and growth.

QUESTIONS FOR REFLECTION

1. How can you collaborate with your colleagues to better support the teaching and learning of multilingual students? What might get in the way? How might you be able to overcome such challenges?
2. What are some ways you can begin to build and sustain positive relationships with the families of your multilingual students?
3. What are ways that you can engage in advocacy for your multilingual students? Their families? The local community?
4. How can self-care help you better support your multilingual students? What are some daily things you can do to manage stress and engage in self-care?

CHAPTER 7

Putting It All Together

In this chapter, we further explore the different ways that the six core practices we have shared in this book can be used to enact humanizing pedagogies in classrooms with multilingual students. We share two additional lesson examples for you to consider and analyze, one from an elementary classroom and the other from a high school classroom. We invite you to explore these examples and identify the core practices present within the lessons, as well as to reflect on what additional core practices for working with multilingual students you might consider integrating throughout the lessons. You may use the Core Practices for Working with Multilingual Students (Table I.1) as well as the Lesson Analysis Templates (Tables 7.1 and 7.2) at the end of this chapter to guide your exploration of the lessons provided (for additional examples to analyze, please look at our video clips about humanizing core practices for multilingual students: https://education.umd.edu/edterps-learning-academy/resources).

ELEMENTARY LESSON: COMMUNITY HELPERS

Erica is a novice ESOL teacher, working at an elementary school in a large urban area. She serves a largely Spanish-speaking population; however, she does not consider her language skills in Spanish to be very strong. During the spring, Erica introduces a new, week-long unit on *Community Helpers* to newcomer learners in her ESOL pull-out classroom. The goals of the unit are for the students to (1) define community helper, (2) identify community helpers (e.g., police officers, firefighters, teachers), and (3) use community helper vocabulary in speech, writing, and reading.

Erica begins the unit with an introductory lesson to define community helpers to five 2nd-grade newcomer learners who have been in the United States for less than 8 months. Erica begins the lesson by greeting each student and checking in to see how they are doing that day. Next, she asks the students what the weather is like that day and helps them respond to the prompt by referring them to a sentence frame (*The weather is_____.*) and weather-related images on a piece of chart paper placed at the front of the room. Next, she reviews different types of pronouns used to describe people (i.e., *she, he, they*) and then quickly moves into the lesson on Community Helpers.

Part 1

Erica begins by presenting the lesson objectives to her students in both Spanish
and English. She displays the written objectives on a piece of laminated paper
and points to each word as students read the objective aloud, in unison.

> *Students:* We will say and write—
> *Erica:* We will say and write. *¿Qué significa?* [What does that mean?]
>   You want to read in Spanish, Linda?
> *Linda: Diremos y escribiremos.* [We will say and write.]
> *Erica:* Oh, *¿diremos y escribiremos qué?* [We will say and write what?]
> *Linda: Los tipos de . . .* [The kinds of . . .]

Linda pauses, not sure how to read the following word. Erica helps her.

> *Erica: Ayudantes.* [Helpers.]
> *Linda: Ayudantes de la comunidad.* [Community helpers.]
> *Erica: Comunidad. Comunidad.* [Community. Community.] So, in
>   English, *otra vez, por favor* [again, please].
> *Students:* We will say and rrrrr—
> *Erica:* Write.
> *Students:* The k-k-
> *Erica:* Kinds.
> *Students:* Kinds.
> *Erica: ¿Qué significa* "kinds?" [What does "kinds" mean?]
> *Linda: Tipos.* [Kinds.]
> *Erica:* Aha.

Erica reads the rest of the objective in English with her students: "The kinds
of community helpers." She continues the lesson by exploring the meaning
of community:

> *Erica:* What is community? What is community? Huh? *¿Qué significa*
>   "community?" [What does "community" mean?]
> *Erica:* (Puts up another poster, with a picture of a city) What is community?
> *Nina: Ciudades.* [Cities.]
> *Erica:* This is a picture of a community. Linda, what is a community?
> *Linda:* The community is the help of students who are speaking Spanish
>   and English.
> *Erica:* Okay, some people in the community, like a teacher helps people
>   to speak English and Spanish. But what is community? (Points to a
>   definition on the poster and reads aloud from it.) "A community is
>   a place where people [points to all the students] live and work." So,
>   community is *comunidad.*

Students: Comunidad.
Erica: Lo mismo. Comunidad. [The same thing. Community.]
Community. *Todos* [Everyone], community.
Students: Community.
Erica: Community.
Students: Community.
Erica: Thank you. What is helper? This says community HELPERS.
¿Qué significa "helper"? [What does "helper" mean?] Helper?
Linda: ¿Comunidad? [Community?]
Erica: Comunidad es community. *Pero* . . . [*Comunidad* is community. But . . .]
Linda: ¿Ayudante? [Helper?]
Erica: Ahhh, helper *es- otra vez?* [Helper is—one more time?]
Linda: Ayudante.
Erica: Ayudante. [Helper.] *Todos* [Everyone], helper.
Students: Helper.
Erica: Helper.
Students: Helper.
Erica: For example, Linda, you are the pencil helper.

Erica hands Linda the pencil cup, and then Linda distributes the pencils.

Erica: Thank you, Linda. Linda is the pencil helper. *Ayudante de* . . . [Helper for . . .]
Nina: Lápiz. [Pencils.]
Erica: (To Linda.) *Gracias* [Thank you.] You can put it back.

The students put their pencils back in the cup.

Erica: Thank you.
Linda: Miss Kraybill is helping for the students put up pencil.
Erica: Yes, Ms. Kraybill is the helper for putting away the pencils. That's right. So, a community helper *es un ayudante de la comunidad, es una persona que ayuda otras personas en la* . . . [is a community helper, is a person who helps others in the . . .]
Linda: Comunidad. [Community.]
Erica: Yes, thank you. Community helpers.

PAUSE AND REFLECT

- What are the different ways that Erica draws upon students' home language as a resource?
- How might you validate students' home languages as resources in your classroom?

Part 2

Erica transitions into the next part of the lesson and shows examples of different pictures and labels of community helpers. She picks up a photo and displays it.

> *Erica:* Who? ¿*Quién?* [Who?] Who is this community helper?
> *Students:* Doctor.
> *Erica:* Oh, doctor. A doctor is a community helper, right?
> *Students:* Yes.
> *Erica:* Yes, HE or SHE?

Students shout out both "he" and "she" as the pronoun corresponding to the image of the doctor in the photograph. Erica points to a chart placed at the front of the room with examples of "he" and "she."

> *Erica:* Remember we have he or she?
> *Students:* SHE.
> *Erica:* SHE. A doctor.

Erica displays another picture.

> *Linda:* ¿*Cartera?* [Mail carrier?]
> *Erica:* Uhuh. Mail . . .
> *Students:* Mail.
> *Erica:* Carrier.
> *Students:* Carrier.
> *Erica:* *Otra vez.* [One more time.] Mail.
> *Students:* Mail.
> *Erica:* Carrier.
> *Students:* Carrier.
> *Erica:* SHE is a mail carrier. A mail carrier is a community helper. An *ayudante* [helper] in the community. Yes.

Erica continues to show the students images of the different community helpers—a teacher, construction worker, firefighter, police officer, and dentist—each time showing the image, asking students to name the community helper, offering support when needed, emphasizing the pronoun that correlates to the image, and providing a brief explanation of what the community helper does. Erica comes to the last two community helper images.

> *Erica:* I have two more. These are a little difficult.
> *Nina:* Tayror.
> *Erica:* (Restates the word.) Tailor. What is she doing?

The students provide different answers all at once.

Erica: She's making clothes, *ropas*, clothes. She's making clothes. This is a tailor. Do you have a tailor in your community?
Linda: My mom in Guatemala is her.
Erica: In Guatemala, your mom . . .
Linda: And my grandma.
Erica: Ah, is a tailor. Okay. They are community helpers. (Holds up a new picture.) This one . . . mechanic.
Students: Mechanic.
Erica: Yeah, mechanic. What does the mechanic do?
Linda: Is with the car, is not working, the making is going and the car working.
Erica: Yes. Bella?
Bella: The car is not working, the mechanic is go.
Erica: Oh, the car is not working, the car cannot go. The mechanic comes to the car and fixes the car. Now the car is working. Thank you, mechanic.
Students: Thank you, mechanic.

PAUSE AND REFLECT

- What are some ways that Erica learns about her students' experiences at home and in their communities through her interactions within the lesson?
- How does Erica attend to both receptive and productive language use in this part of the lesson?
- How does Erica scaffold students' understanding of what a community helper is?
- What are some ways you could promote students' receptive and productive language use in your classroom?

Part 3

Erica then puts up new posters that feature additional community helpers. She pulls out a book and displays it for students to see the title, *Helpers in My Community*.

Erica: These are the community helpers. This says helpers. *¿Qué significa* "helpers"? [What does "helpers" mean?]
Students: *Ayudantes.* [Helpers.]
Erica: Ah. Helpers . . . (Points to the title.)
Students: In my *comunidad* [community].
Erica: Yes, helpers in my community.

Students: En mi comunidad. [In my community.]
Erica: Aha.

Together they look at each person on the cover of the book, naming their profession: doctor, veterinarian, and firefighter. Erica opens the book to the first page and asks the students to identify the appropriate pronoun for the construction worker presented on the page:

Erica: He or she?
Students: HE.
Erica: ¿Qué? [What?]
Students: SHE.
Erica: She is a . . .
Linda: Ella. [She.]
Erica: She is a construction worker. She is a construction worker.
Maria: My uncle is working in the construction.
Erica: Your uncle is a construction worker? Oh, he is a construction worker.

Bella points to the picture and notes that her dad is a construction worker.

Erica: Your dad, he is a construction worker. Oh, anyone else? Yes.
Linda: My dad is color the house and my mom . . .
Erica: Your dad paints the house.
Linda: And my mom.
Erica: Oh, okay. Okay.

Nina also shares that her dad works on houses, too.

Erica: Oh, he is the, what do you call that? Contractor.
Nina: Yes.

Erica turns through a few pages, skipping some of the community helpers who have already been discussed. She comes to the page with a doctor.

Nina: He is a doctor.
Erica: He? (Looks confused.)
Nina: He is a doctor.
Erica: HE? (Looks more visibly confused.)
Students: SHE!
Erica: She is a doctor.
Nina: A school doctor.
Erica: Or school nurse. What is nurse?

Nina: The doctor is office.
Erica: Yeah, we have a nurse.

Several students begin to talk at the same time about the nurse's office and then they discuss the third person in the picture:

Erica: This is a crossing guard. Like, like Miss Kraybill in *la tarde* [the afternoon]. Miss Kraybill stands with the walkie talkie, you know? And I say, "Okay, bus, you can go. You stop, this one coming."
Linda: You help with the *comunidad* [community].
Erica: Yes, I'm a community helper. I am a crossing guard in the afternoon at the school.
María: (Says something quietly.)
Erica: Say what?
María: (Repeats, almost inaudibly.)
Erica: (Excitedly.) You want to be a doctor when you are big? Oh, I like that! You will be a good doctor, María.

Erica continues to turn pages and the students identify the names of the community helpers, as well as their pronouns. On one page, there are multiple firefighters. The students identify the male firefighter and state that his pronoun should be "he." Erica points to the group of the firefighters and asks the students:

Erica: He?
Students: They
Erica: They IS? (She points to "are" in "They are" sentence frame located at the front of the classroom.)
Students: They are firefighters.
Erica: Oh, THEY ARE firefighters. (Turns the page.)
Students: Police.
Erica: Police. He? She? They?
Students: They.
Bella: He and she.
Erica: Aha. I should turn this one around. (Erica turns around another sentence frame, which reads "He/she is a_____.") We can say, for example (pointing to the sentence strip), he is a . . . (Points to picture.)
Students: Police.
Erica: Police officer. Or, *los dos* [the two]?
Nina: They.
Erica: They are police officers. They are police officers. Okay.

Erica closes the book and explains that the students will now be making sentences through verbal discussion with one another.

PAUSE AND REFLECT

- What are some practices that Erica uses to support vocabulary development?
- In what ways does Erica use comprehensible input in this segment of the lesson?
- Does Erica's lesson support the content and language objectives presented? If so, how?
- How might you support students' vocabulary development and offer comprehensible input in your classroom?

Questions to Consider

- What core practices are represented throughout the elementary lesson?
- What additional core practices might you include in the lesson?
- What aspects of the lesson are humanizing?
- What additional strategies might you include to further humanize the pedagogy in this lesson?

SECONDARY LESSON: COLLABORATIVE PROTOCOLS

Melissa teaches language arts to 9th- and 10th-grade multilingual students at a large, urban high school that serves only multilingual learners. The majority of her students are Spanish-speaking and have emigrated from countries throughout Central America. Ms. Nahmias is a student teacher in Melissa's classroom.

This lesson takes place during early spring. Melissa's students are halfway through a reading unit on culture shock and cultural differences. In upcoming lessons, students will be placed in leveled reading groups and assigned specific roles, so Melissa focuses on two lessons that center on collaborative protocols to prepare them for the different roles that will be required in their upcoming group work. The focus of this lesson is for students to practice the different roles while engaging in a collaborative activity—building a marshmallow tower.

Part 1

Melissa begins class by sharing a "Friday Funny," a 2-minute video of ducks chasing cats and dogs, while she takes attendance. She then collects homework from students and moves into the learning objectives for the day: "Students will form groups and work together to assign roles, establish expectations, and make a plan." She begins by asking students to quickly discuss two key terms: collaboration and cooperation.

Melissa: I want you guys to take 2 minutes to discuss what do you think the difference between collaboration and cooperation is. Kasandra, can you help me out? What are these words in Spanish?

Kasandra: Colaboración y cooperación. [Collaboration and cooperation.]

Melissa: Okay, so take 2 minutes. You're going to talk in your group, you can even jot down some notes on the back of your group paper, and then I'm going to write some of your ideas up on the board.

Melissa sets a timer video with music for 2 minutes. She moves from group to group actively listening to students discuss these two terms. After 2 minutes, Melissa calls the students to attention and they report out their conversations and discuss what collaboration and cooperation mean. Melissa connects the terms to the learning objectives for the day:

Melissa: So what we're going to be doing today is we're going to be getting ourselves set up (points to vocabulary words on board) to collaborate on a project, because we will not all be doing the same thing to meet our goal. Does that make sense? So, we're going to learn about what the different jobs are that we're going to do for our goal today. But, you're in new situations and we've been working together recently in pairs, or we were working in mixed groups, big groups for Jenga, then we were in pairs for our partner interviews. So now you're working in new groups, and we want to give you a grade on how well you guys have been working together.

Melissa turns her attention to the rubric displayed on the board and reminds students that this rubric for collaboration is also used in their health class. She explains how to earn the number of points associated with each proficiency level—Beginning (1), Developing (2), Proficient (2.5), and Wow Work! (3)—and shares a brief video montage of popular movie clips that demonstrate examples of each level of collaboration in the rubric. She gives directions for getting started:

Melissa: Okay, so here's what we're gonna do. We are going to start doing our collaborative protocol. Ms. Nahmias (the student teacher) is going to come around and give you guys our collaborative graphic organizer. There are five steps that we're going to use. Today, we're only going to get through the first four steps, okay? And then Ms. Nahmias will also be giving you guys group role cards. So, we have five group roles. Can I get a reader if someone thinks they can do all five? Okay, Kasandra. Can you just read the names of all five group roles?

Kasandra: "Facilitator. Recorder. Timekeeper. File manager. Communicator."

Melissa: Okay, Alistair, what is the facilitator's job?

Alistair: "To tell members of the group what they are supposed to be doing."

Melissa: Okay, Emerson, what does a recorder do?

Emerson: "Takes notes and writes down the most important point."

After going over all five roles in this manner, Melissa asks students to discuss possible role assignments in their groups:

Melissa: Talk to each other. You might think about your strengths and your weaknesses. Someone who might not feel like they have the best handwriting, maybe you don't want to start off by being the recorder, but you really feel confident in your speaking, maybe you want to be the communicator.

The students talk about who should assume which role, and Melissa and Ms. Nahmias move from group to group, listening and asking questions. Melissa arrives at Kasandra's group, who completed the task quickly:

Melissa: You already decided on group roles. How did you decide so fast?

Kasandra: Because we have already done this with the health teacher.

Melissa: Okay. So Kasandra, why did you decide to be the facilitator and the recorder?

Kasandra: Because I like to maintain everything in order, like organizing the group. That's why I wanted to take those.

Melissa: Oh nice. Are you guys okay with her taking those two roles?

Students: Yeah.

Melissa: Okay, Liliana, why do you want to be timekeeper?

Liliana: Because I will support my group members to do their work.

Melissa: (To the rest of the group.) Are we cool with Liliana being timekeeper?

Kasandra: Yes.

Melissa: And Valeria, why did you choose file manager?

Valeria: I dunno.

Melissa: You don't know? Do you know what the file manager needs to do?

Valeria reads the role card.

Valeria: To organize the materials.

Melissa: Yeah, so at the end of class when I say I need my cards back, you're gonna give me my cards. We okay with Valeria doing that job? (To Wilfredo.) Okay, how about you, communicator?

> *Wilfredo:* Because I like to ask questions to you and you give me answers.
>
> *Melissa:* So when you run into trouble, what are you gonna do, Wilfredo?
>
> *Wilfredo:* I'm gonna tell you.
>
> *Melissa:* And you're gonna ask me. All right, sounds good. Nice job!

After a few minutes, Melissa calls the class to attention with a call and response procedure:

> *Melissa:* All right, everyone, PHOENIX!
>
> *Students:* United.
>
> *Melissa:* PHOENIX!
>
> *Students:* (More loudly.) UNITED!
>
> *Melissa:* Okay, it seems like we're ready, so we're gonna move to the next step.

PAUSE AND REFLECT

- What are some practices that Melissa uses to support vocabulary development?
- How does Melissa work to create a positive learning environment with clear procedures, consistent routines, and high expectations?
- How might you teach the procedures for an activity like this in your classroom?

Part 2

Melissa stands at the front of the class next to her computer, and advances the slides for the PowerPoint presentation. She begins by encouraging students to think about the agreements they will need for successful group work:

> *Melissa:* We should all have a recorder now, so the recorder's gonna be the one writing the ideas of the group. That does not mean they are the one coming up with the ideas. So, we need to make an agreement. You guys are gonna have a task that I will reveal at the end of class. You don't know what it is, but you have to think, if we have to do something on paper, something maybe creative with art. If we have to do something on the computer, what agreements do we need that will help us work well together? So now we want to think about our weaknesses. So maybe we get a little tempted by our cell phone. We're feeling really sleepy in seventh period after lunch. So, you're going to write down what you're going to agree

on as a group that you guys will do or will not do so you can work well together.

She gives students some examples for group rules they could write.

> *Melissa:* So, for example, "We will stay in our seats and get the work done." If you have someone who wants to walk around the room, that might be a good agreement. "We will talk in an indoor voice." Maybe you have somebody in your group who's really loud, likes to scream and shout, and you think, "Oh, okay, so maybe no cell phones? No computers?" Talk to each other. Think about your weaknesses and come up with agreements that you need to be successful.

Melissa asks the students to collaborate in their teams to come up with agreements that they need to be successful. She circulates the classroom and checks in with different groups.

> *Melissa:* All right, guys, what else might we need?
> *Marco:* No headphones.
> *Melissa:* No headphones.
> *Cynthia:* No electronic devices.
> *Melissa:* You can put "and headphones." No phones and headphones. You can make it one.
> *Cynthia:* You can say no phones, no headphones, no computer.
> *Melissa:* But we might need it, though. What if I have a Google Doc that you're collaborating on? So what rule might you need if you had the computers out? So let's say you're supposed to be typing on a Google Doc, but one person is watching soccer on their computer.
> *Marco:* No YouTube.
> *Melissa:* So maybe no YouTube.

Melissa continues to move to new groups and talk about the different types of agreements the groups are creating. She reminds the whole class they have 20 seconds to finish their discussions and then calls time:

> *Melissa:* All right, guys, that is time. Phoenix!
> *Wilfredo:* UNITED.
> *Melissa:* Thank you, Wilfedo. PHOENIX!
> *Students:* UNITED.
> *Melissa:* All right, guys, so really quickly, can I get some examples of some of our agreements? So, Alistair, what is an agreement you guys have? Just one.
> *Alistair:* Using only English.

Melissa: Using only English. Why do you need that agreement?

Alistair: Because if we only speak English, we can understand each other more.

Melissa: Yeah, do you all speak the same language?

Alistair: No.

Melissa: No, so you need English. Damario, what did you all come up with? Just one.

Damario: No use the cell phone in class.

Melissa: Why no cell phone?

Damario: Because it's a distraction.

Melissa: Good, oh who wants to answer for your team? Amelio.

Amelio: Don't sleep in the classroom.

Melissa: Why do we need to not sleep during the group work?

Amelio: Because you will not understand what is the teacher says when you do the project work.

Melissa: You might not remember. Okay, Kasandra. (To students in the group.) Is it okay if Kasandra speaks for your group?

Kasandra: Support each other. Because when someone does not understand, we can explain to them and help them.

Melissa: Good. Very nice.

PAUSE AND REFLECT

- How does Melissa help to build community in this lesson?
- What types of opportunities for receptive and productive language use are present in the lesson?
- What might you do in your classroom to build community and develop your students' social-emotional skills?

Part 3

Melissa flips to the next PowerPoint slide and explains to the students that in the upcoming project they will be working together to see which team can create the tallest tower made of spaghetti and miniature marshmallows. She reviews several important questions about the upcoming assignment and then asks students to begin to sketch out a plan for constructing their marshmallow tower in their small groups.

Melissa: So we have given you guys a graphic organizer where you could decide, "what's my step one? What's my step two?" Remember our goal is to make our marshmallow tower, or you could draw a picture on the back. Now our goal is to make the tallest tower, so is this tallest or is this tallest? (Melissa holds up her hands to show horizontal or vertical.) This is tallest (holds hands up and down to demonstrate vertical), okay, so it has to stay standing. So we have about 5 minutes. I want you guys to start thinking about how you guys can achieve the tallest tower. Okay?

Melissa passes out graphic organizers and students begin to discuss and plan in their small groups over the next 5 minutes, while Melissa rotates between groups:

Melissa: (Asking one group.) So what do you guys think might be the best first step for winning the tower contest?
Silvestre: Put first four marshmallows.
Melissa: Jordan, do you agree with that? So make sure everybody in the group is listening. So four marshmallows, do you think that's enough? Do you think that'll be strong enough?
Jordan: Maybe six?
Melissa: That's perfect. And you'll have about 30 pieces of spaghetti. Are we writing down? It seems like you have some good ideas. Are you writing it down? Or drawing it?

Melissa calls time for the students and she wraps up the lesson for the day.

PAUSE AND REFLECT

- What are some ways that Melissa scaffolds instruction for her learners?
- How might Melissa use informal assessment to make sure students understand the expectations?
- Does Melissa's lesson support the content and language objectives presented? If so, how?

QUESTIONS TO CONSIDER

- What core practices are represented throughout the lesson?
- What additional core practices might you include in the lesson?
- What aspects of the lesson are humanizing?
- What additional strategies might you include to further humanize pedagogy?

Table 7.1. Lesson Analysis Template I

Teacher:		Lesson:
Core Practices		**Analytic Notes**
CP Present? (✓ if yes)	**Which one?**	
Reflections:		

Table 7.2. Lesson Analysis Template II

Core Practices	Evidence

Knowing Students

- Home language
- Home literacy
- English language
- English literacy
- Prior schooling
- Interests
- Experiences at home and in the community

Learning Environment

- Clear procedures
- Consistent routines
- High expectations
- Social-emotional learning
- Culturally and linguistically responsive and sustaining pedagogies

Content and Language Instruction

- Comprehensible input
- Scaffolding
- Differentiation
- Content and language objectives

Language and Literacy Development

- Promoting vocabulary development
- Using students' home language/knowledge as a resource
- Prioritizing receptive and productive language skills
- Adapting instruction based on students' linguistic needs

Assessment

- Using formal and informal assessment appropriately and fairly
- Utilizing standardized and formal tests to design appropriate instruction
- Differentiating formal and informal assessment

Relationships and Advocacy

- Collaborating with colleagues
- Collaborating with families
- Engaging in advocacy
- Practicing self-care

CHAPTER 8

Humanizing the Teaching Experience
Challenges and Solutions

Developing humanizing teaching that embraces who multilingual students are as whole human beings, while also challenging inequities in their education, is demanding work, and you need allies and thought partners to support you. It is important to find ways of working that affirm you, challenge you, and help you keep growing. Our long-term collaborative research project, which took place outside the school day and outside specific school and district structures and requirements, afforded our team opportunities to engage in experiences that are not typically part of teachers' day-to-day work. The teachers in our group had the opportunity to collaborate with us and with each other over an extended period of time, both during and after they left the teacher certification program that they were enrolled in with the teacher educators and researchers on this team. They also had the opportunity to grapple with big questions about how they were engaging in practice, and to analyze and discuss instruction and other aspects of their work as teachers.

The teachers noted that such opportunities are not regularly part of their school conversations or district-based professional development. However, we believe that with intention, there are aspects of our collaboration that could be incorporated into schools' existing formats to help humanize the teaching experience of teachers, which is critical if teachers are also going to be humanizing practitioners themselves. Here we share some of the school and district structural challenges that emerged in our work as being dehumanizing for teachers, and some possible solutions that we had the opportunity to try, or that teachers suggested as solutions to work against these structural challenges (see also Table 8.1).

TEACHER AUTONOMY

In many cases, teachers lack autonomy in their schools and classrooms to make decisions about what is most responsive to their students as unique individuals. Our experience together has shown us that it can be beneficial to create smaller groups of teachers who want to examine particular instructional, curricular, or structural issues. So can enabling teachers to create such groups themselves, and these may span content areas, grade levels, and different schools. The teachers in our group greatly appreciated the opportunity to talk to teachers in other grades, content areas, schools, and even districts, and felt they were enriched by hearing about a range of ideas. For instance, Andrew shared:

> Being a part of a reflective, problem-solving team has helped me become more analytical about my practice as a teacher. I find that I am thinking more about how I am teaching content and language to my students. I'm asking myself more questions such as, "What was successful about a lesson? Why? What would have made it better?" As busy teachers, I think it is very easy to plan a lesson, teach it, and move on without giving it much thought; but being a part of this group has encouraged me to be more reflective and proactive about how I teach.

The teachers in our group also wanted more opportunities to make decisions about their curriculum, instruction, and assessment, as Erica suggested:

> How do you make space for higher performing teachers, those more out-of-the-box thinking teachers, the ones who are willing to put in the work, but don't necessarily feel like the system knows the best way to address all their students' individual needs, and they need the freedom to be able to do that?

Erica suggested that allowing teachers more freedom to develop curriculum and pacing that is more responsive to their students would allow teachers to better support students' learning. Teachers can also find ways to meet with small groups of colleagues who want to examine particular instructional, curricular, or structural issues, and present possible solutions to their administrators. Since schools are hierarchies where power is unequally distributed, and a single teacher may feel powerless to make changes in their school context, finding allies who are willing to push an issue together can make it easier to address structural inequities in multilingual students' education.

TIME

Most teachers feel there is not enough time in the day to cover everything they would like. However, teachers of multilingual students often feel even more constrained by lack of time than teachers who do not regularly work with multilingual learners. In part, this is because teachers of multilingual students need time to coordinate with other teachers, so that the work they do with students aligns well with the grade-level curriculum and pacing that is occurring in other classrooms, providing maximum support for multilingual students. Another reason that teachers of multilingual students feel more pressed for time is because of the lack of appropriate materials and curriculum that differentiates and scaffolds in ways that draw on multilingual students' resources, while also supporting their content learning and language development. Thus, teachers can frequently find themselves taking time to create or adapt their own materials, making them more responsive to their particular learner groups. As Chris shared:

> My stress has been the planning. I'm just exhausted from planning. I've been frustrated that I don't have a unit plan where we're working toward something for the entire unit. We have this document that says, "First quarter: Past tense" and, like, "Adverbs and adjectives." This is literally all it says. There's a column that says: "Unit 1, do past tense."

And Nancy noted how much she changed the ELA curriculum provided by her district and how much time she spent modifying it:

> I don't follow the pacing that it sets. I mean, why start the year with informational writing, like with speeches, when you could more easily start with narratives, and build that background for your kids, build those writing and reading skills with something that's content-wise a little easier for them to understand? The curriculum is not ESOL-friendly. At all. I completely flipped it (putting narratives first and informational text last).

We have learned that teachers and their students benefit from schedules and planning time that allow teachers to collaborate more frequently. For instance, some school systems have a half day once a week with the afternoon set aside for teachers' collaborative planning. Finding ways to release teachers during the school day, or pay them for extra time after school or in the summer, offers an opportunity for teachers to work collaboratively. All of the teachers in our group have taken advantage of these opportunities when they arise. Kendall, Erica, Andrea, and some of their colleagues at school have focused on planning together, and their principal has offered opportunities for them to observe in other teachers' classrooms in their school. Andrea shared:

> I like to be able to use our colleagues as our professional learning community, to be able to just walk into somebody else's classroom, watch for a few minutes, and have a conversation. And I think that comes from building trust, building relationships. And it takes time, we have to spend time building those relationships. But I can build a connection at work. That's improving both of our practices as teachers.

Melissa also noted that her high school frequently invited teachers and administrators from other schools to observe and learn in classrooms at her school, that they regularly shared materials with each other and across her district, and that she and her colleagues benefitted from being paid in the summer to collaborate and generate new materials together.

Teaching multilingual students often presents challenges for teachers' personal time. Teachers often spend significant extra time outside the school day planning, grading, and thinking about their teaching and their students. As we discussed in Chapter 6, to be an effective teacher, you need to have time to recharge and maintain other interests and time for loved ones. A strategy Melissa uses is to have a yoga class she wants to get to in the afternoon, which serves as a reminder to make her leave her school building by a certain time. Andrea explained that she needed to remember that she isn't an island, and is part of a team who cares about her:

> Thankfully, at my school we have administrators who have excellent support for the staff—when we need personal time, when there's anything going on outside of work in our lives. Not only do they make themselves aware of it, but they tell us, "Take care of yourself first." And they'll follow up and they'll ask us, "How is that thing going at home? What's going on with your family?" And you can tell that they are genuine and they really care.

Nancy similarly commented that she needed to remember to ask for help when she felt overwhelmed:

> I need to recognize when I need to reach out to people. I have a huge network of support at school, and so this week I reached out to individual people about sharing some of my responsibilities at school. I think that's going to be my strategy moving forward: communicating when I need a break.

However, there are also times when teachers do not feel supported. In her first year teaching, Erica shared that:

> I don't have as much support as I would like. It's not coming from my principal. I feel like I'm figuring it out on my own.

And Chris noted a similar challenge:

> I think it's more important than ever for educators to communicate that most of us are not given the time and resources necessary to do everything that we are asked to do. We have to make choices and set limits, or we will burn out.

It is important to make sure that you self-advocate for not being given more duties than other teachers (e.g., lunch, recess, student support, testing proctor, clubs, and enrichment). Help your colleagues and administrators understand what your work with multilingual students involves. When you think that students will benefit from collaborative planning and/or teaching, try to illustrate to administrators why this is the case, and advocate for time and mechanisms (tools, routines, job responsibilities) that make collaboration possible without adding significant additional planning and assessment time to your workload.

COMMUNICATION AND COORDINATION

Many different stakeholders and factors contribute to the learning and development of multilingual students, including ESOL teachers, content area teachers, school administrators, school counselors, other school specialists, district curriculum specialists, district assessment specialists, state boards of education, federal laws and requirements for the education of multilingual students, and of course, students' own families and communities. Given the number and variety of people, offices, policies, and procedures involved, it is often difficult to have communication, agreement, and alignment among all the different entities, and it is inevitable that there will be decisions that conflict with one another. For instance, TC observed that a new policy at her school had resulted in a number of newcomer students being placed at a level that was too demanding for them:

> I went to the other teachers, and I went to the counselor, and I was like, "Something's not right, I don't know if this is the right place for them." I put in a request with the counselor. I had to go down and see the team lead, and explain to them, "This student wants to be moved, she wants to be somewhere where she understands."

As TC's anecdote illustrates, such situations may call upon you and others to offer input and advocacy, to help other parties involved to see the whole picture of multilingual students' academic experience. Where possible, it is helpful to infuse teacher, family, student, and community member voices and input in district and school decision-making. Invite a variety of stakeholders to be members of groups that steer and guide what happens in schools and districts. Create a regular mechanism for these stakeholder groups to offer feedback to school and district decision-makers—such as meetings with ESOL department heads, district level ESOL meetings, grade-level planning meetings that ESOL specialists attend, weekly informal meetings with parents, and parent advisory councils—and use this feedback to make meaningful policies, decisions, and changes.

ASSESSMENT

While it is important to use assessment to gain a good understanding of multilingual students' existing language and content knowledge (see Chapter 5), and to get to know more about your students (see Chapter 1) so that you can create the best possible instruction for them (see Chapter 3), there is frequently a lot of emphasis on assessing multilingual students, and much of this assessment can be frightening and frustrating to students, rather than supporting their learning. Kendall expressed frustration with the many standardized assessments in which her students were required to participate:

> I feel like all the assessments are a waste of resources and energy and people, and I don't feel effective. Students sit there like a deer in the headlights and they don't know how to answer the test questions and they don't know how to start. They all just sit there and stare at the screen. Their scores on the language proficiency test are not always a true reflection of their proficiency levels. Especially for the speaking section on the test, they get very nervous and clam up. And so I know that their speaking scores are artificially low a lot of times and not reflective of their true abilities.

Other teachers in our group agreed, and noted that because many of the assessments their multilingual students are required to take are in English, which may not accurately measure the students' knowledge due to their language proficiency (see Chapter 5), the students often felt "freaked out," "overwhelmed," and "unsuccessful."

While there may be limited influence you can have over testing calendars and assessment requirements, you can help by building your colleagues' and your own assessment literacy. For example, learn whether assessments have been tested with student populations including multilingual students (this information is often available on the test publisher's website); have discussions about what assessment accommodations are most helpful for students while maintaining the integrity of the assessment; and ask for opportunities for classroom teachers and ESOL specialists to collaborate when interpreting assessment information.

PROFESSIONAL DEVELOPMENT

Teachers often feel that the professional development opportunities provided by their districts are not sufficiently tailored to questions they have about their own teaching, learner population, and dilemmas. They also feel that when they get busy at school, they focus on getting through the day and do not have many opportunities to focus on their continued learning and development. We have found that when teachers have opportunities to get together about their own problems of practice, they are truly excited about what they can learn and accomplish together. We learned that when teachers have school-based opportunities for professional development, and teachers are allowed to identify areas for inquiry and growth, they are very motivated and generate a lot of learning and ideas together. For instance, TC shared the following comment about our work together:

This group has really helped me figure out what my end game is, like what kind of a teacher I want to become. I want to continue to learn, I don't want to be that teacher with all this experience and set in my ways. I want to continue to be humble and learn from my fellow teachers. This group has really helped me with growing, and not only as a teacher, but emotionally, too, being able to know where I want to be overall.

And Stephanie noted:

After our meetings, I have more energy in my own motivation to grow in my practice due to the sense of community that the project builds. Being able to talk about issues that impact ESOL teachers with teachers who all have different perspectives is refreshing and inspiring, and has helped me grow in my own practice. The conversations and questions that the project initiates give me the chance to expand my thoughts or make changes and question my own practices more readily.

We suggest that districts could put funds used for outside professional development efforts toward these more localized opportunities.

We also learned that teachers really appreciate opportunities to observe other teachers and classrooms and engage in structured, but not evaluative, conversation about their teaching. The teachers in our group enjoyed having a chance to observe colleagues in action and learn from them. Erica shared how valuable this was for her as she was developing as a teacher:

I've had the opportunity to be in many different classrooms. My first year teaching ESOL, I worked with four different teachers and spent about an equal amount of time in their different classrooms. There's a lot of stuff that you notice. There was one teacher in particular, her classroom ran so smoothly, you walked in, her students always knew exactly what to do, where to be. But what was interesting to me was at the beginning of the year she spent the first week or two teaching the students routines and procedures. Having the benefit of seeing other teachers do that, over the course of years, and seeing how it pays off for them, has been really beneficial for me.

Furthermore, the teachers in our group felt strongly about how important it is to support new teachers through nonevaluative, welcoming spaces that allow them to express doubts and challenges about their teaching, and to problem solve, without judgment. The teachers expressed that our group was a "safe space" where they could reflect on their practice and their experiences and be "very honest" without fear of negative repercussions. While they noted that their usual observations and conversations at school with administrators about their teaching are more evaluative, they are excited when they have an opportunity to talk about their teaching in places where they feel safe sharing their doubts, concerns, and dilemmas. They felt that our team provided such a space and appreciated opportunities to meet and talk about their teaching questions. Andrew shared:

> Even though I work with a team of teachers and I am surrounded by students all day, it often feels like the obstacles, concerns, and frustrations that I encounter are unique to me. I've enjoyed having the chance to hear from other ESOL teachers about their experiences. It helps me realize that I'm not alone in my challenges, and it gives me a sense of community with my colleagues.

Kendall noted something similar about her experience of being part of our team:

> This has been a great resource. This group has this very shared experience that you can get insights from that other people just don't have to offer. And hearing people say, "Oh, I made it through this," or "I experienced this," and hearing how they handled things and strategies and solutions and being able to workshop issues that you're encountering, it's really nice.

One way we suggest supporting teachers' continued growth is to leverage existing partnerships between area universities and school systems to create collaboration that benefits teachers and students. We suggest using professional development schools, mentor/student teacher relationships, and school- and classroom-based studies as opportunities to connect, engage, and solve problems collaboratively. Use identified problems of practice from teachers, administrators, families, and students to help drive collaborative efforts to study and improve them. Find ways to involve teachers at the university, and university faculty in the schools.

Our project together has created one such way to do this. Finding opportunities to engage in research-practice partnerships, or initiatives that engage school- and district-based personnel in joint work with university personnel to identify and address real problems of practice, is a great way to do this. The teachers in our group felt that their geographic proximity and their ongoing relationships with the university where they received their teaching degree provided significant benefit for their continued growth and exposure to new ideas. They had opportunities to participate in classroom- and school-based research projects led by university faculty and graduate students as well as to host student teachers in their classrooms, which they noted were both exciting ways to continue learning about and incorporating the latest ideas in teaching

Table 8.1. Supporting Teachers' Humanizing Practice

Challenges to Humanizing Practice	Teacher Solutions	Administrator Solutions
Lack of teacher autonomy to make decisions and use a curriculum that is responsive to students as unique individuals.	Find ways to meet with small groups of colleagues who want to examine particular instructional, curricular, or structural issues.	Support teachers in creating smaller groupings themselves, which may sometimes span content areas, grade levels, and different schools. Give experienced and impactful teachers more time and autonomy to make decisions about curriculum, instruction, and assessment.
Lack of time to create materials and consult with colleagues in ways that allow teachers to better support multilingual students.	Create tools and processes for collaborating with colleagues (shared folders, documents, quick check-ins).	Create schedules and planning time that allow teachers to collaborate more frequently. Find ways to release teachers during the school day, or pay them for extra time after school and/or in the summer.
Excessive demands on teachers' time, which limits time to recharge and have other interests and time for loved ones.	Make sure that you self-advocate for not being given more duties than other teachers (e.g., lunch, recess, student support, testing proctor, clubs, and enrichment).	Visit and talk with teachers of multilingual students to understand their day-to-day demands. Support teachers' needs for rest and renewal.
Lack of communication and coordination across different groups who support the curriculum, instruction, and assessment of multilingual students.	Invite family members, colleagues, and administrators to your classroom to observe, participate in, and contribute to classroom activities.	Infuse teacher, family, student, and community member voices and input in district and school decision-making. Invite them to be members of groups that steer and guide what happens in schools and districts.

(continued)

Table 8.1. Supporting Teachers' Humanizing Practice (*continued*)

Challenges to Humanizing Practice	Teacher Solutions	Administrator Solutions
		Create a regular mechanism for these stakeholder groups to offer feedback to school and district decision-makers, and use this feedback to make meaningful changes.
Excessive assessment of multilingual students, which may be on topics and at a language level inappropriate for multilingual students and take away from instructional time and opportunities to get to know students.	Build your own and your colleagues' assessment literacy.	Question and examine the validity of assessments and consider how many are necessary.
Limited opportunities for continued growth, including professional development that is top-down rather than teacher-initiated.	Work with colleagues to discuss problems of practice and identify what resources (materials, people, tools) would best allow you to address those problems. Observe your colleagues and use this as an opportunity to discuss questions you have about teaching and learning. Stay connected to area universities: participate in events and professional development they offer, host student teachers in your classroom, consider participating in research projects.	Offer school-based opportunities for professional development. Allow teachers to identify areas for inquiry and growth. Put funds used for outside professional development efforts toward these more localized opportunities. Create opportunities for teachers to observe other teachers and classrooms and engage in structured, but not evaluative, conversation about their teaching. Leverage existing partnerships between area universities and school systems to create collaboration that benefits teachers and students.

and learning. Melissa shared: "Interns bring in new perspectives, and I always want to know, 'What are you hearing? What are you learning?'" Likewise, teacher education students and faculty at the university benefit from ongoing collaborations with area schools, staying abreast of the latest district initiatives and changes in demographics. This also allows university preparation and research on teacher education for multilingual students to more closely align with the realities of local schools.

We believe that if district and school leaders understand and recognize that these factors help to humanize teachers and the teaching experience, and that they help teachers to better humanize their practice and support the achievement of multilingual students, this can go a long way in creating more humanizing teaching and learning experiences.

HOW SHOULD I START BUILDING MY HUMANIZING PRACTICE?

Start small by approaching parts of the core practices described in this book instead of trying to do it all at once. Start with one or two of our core practices and think about how you already use them in your teaching, and how you can further develop them. Remember that these core practices should help you reflect on your practice, and they are not intended to be evaluative. Find like-minded colleagues and work together. Try to get involved in groups that help you look critically at your teaching and grow as a teacher, while also supporting you and allowing you space to ask questions, share ideas, and express your doubts. Teacher educators, and researchers at universities and leaders and administrators in districts also need to find ways to advocate for developing environments that are responsive to teachers and students, if teachers are going to engage in humanizing practice. It is difficult to expect humanizing practice from teachers if the larger systems they are part of make it challenging. Know that you cannot change the systemic issues alone. However, you can encourage your colleagues, administrators, community members, and other stakeholders to consider the impact that more humanizing approaches can have on teachers, teaching, and students, and you can urge them to strive to create more humanizing educational spaces, interactions, and systems. As Andrea said to us:

> I love teaching. I love learning how to teach better. It's like this never-ending puzzle or quest. I love solving puzzles and teaching is just a giant puzzle to me, and I think it always will be, so the work will always be there.

Indeed, this work will always be there, and we hope it is exciting for you. We hope that the core practices we have developed and discussed in this book help you on your own quest, and that your capacity for humanizing the teaching and learning experiences for multilingual students—and their teachers, families, and communities—continues to grow. We appreciate you taking this important journey with us.

QUESTIONS FOR REFLECTION

- What core practices are you already using in your teaching? What evidence from your practice do you have of using those practices? Are you using them in humanizing ways? How do you know?
- What core practices would you like to work on? How do you think you might get started?
- Do you have a group of colleagues you can connect with to reflect on humanizing your practice? How might you create or build on that?
- What goals do you have for your teaching after reading this book?

Additional Resources

INTRODUCTION

The following texts provide additional important insights regarding humanizing pedagogy, why it is important, and how teachers do it:

- Howard, G. (2016). *We can't teach what we don't know: White teachers, multiracial schools* (3rd ed.). Teachers College Press.
- Ladson-Billings, G. (1994). *The dreamkeepers: Successful teachers of African American children.* Jossey-Bass.
- National Education Association. (2012). *English Language Learners: Culture, equity and language.* https://www.youtube.com/watch?v=5HU80AxmP-U

Figure A.1. Core Practices for teaching multilingual students.

CORE PRACTICES
for teaching multilingual students

KNOWING STUDENTS
Learn students' histories and experiences in and out of school. Consider students' home languages and literacies, English language and literacy, prior schooling experiences, interests, and home and community assets.

LEARNING ENVIRONMENT
Build a positive learning environment that has clear procedures, consistent routines, and high expectations that support culturally and linguistically responsive and sustaining pedagogies, and social-emotional skills.

CONTENT & LANGUAGE INSTRUCTION
Plan and enact content and language instruction in ways that meet students at their current level. Use comprehensible input, scaffolding, differentiation, and integrated content and language objectives to foster knowledge and language growth.

LANGUAGE & LITERACY DEVELOPMENT
Support students' language and literacy development by using home languages as a resource, promoting vocabulary development in the content areas, and prioritizing receptive and productive language skills.

ASSESSMENT
Develop assessments that are attentive to students' language proficiency, and use assessment to inform instruction. Be mindful to match content and language objectives with the learning demands and to differentiate assessments to accommodate students' ability levels.

RELATIONSHIPS AND ADVOCACY
Build relationships of dignity, care, and respect with colleagues, families, and yourself. Engage in advocacy to support students, families, and communities.

- Nieto, S. (2014). *Why we teach now.* Teachers College Press.
- Sensoy, Ö. & DiAngelo, R. (2017). *Is everyone really equal? An introduction to key concepts in social justice education* (2nd ed.). Teachers College Press.

CHAPTER 1

These resources, assignments, and activities offer some ways to get to know your students:

Where I'm from poems:

Have students write poetry to help them express who they are.

- Jones, S. (2006). *Girls, social class, and literacy: What teachers can do to make a difference.* Heinemann.
- Lyon, G. E. (1999). *Where I'm from: Where poems come from.* Absey.

Heart maps:

Students use a heart map template to fill with images and words about their most important people, places, and things.

- Heard, G. (2016). *Heart maps: Helping students create and craft authentic writing.* Heinemann.

Ask me about:

Provide a set of cue cards with topics such as family, foods, TV shows, hobbies, games, pets, celebrations. As Wager and colleagues describe, students choose three cards they are willing to talk about and the class asks them questions about these topics.

- Wager, A. C., Clarke, L. W., & Enriquez, G. (2019). *The reading turn-around with emergent bilinguals: A five-part framework for powerful teaching and learning (grades K–6).* Teachers College Press.

Life events timeline:

Students create a timeline with 5–7 important events in their lives indicated through images or writing.

- For directions, see https://www.colorincolorado.org/article/using-timelines-enhance-comprehension

Funds of knowledge:

Understanding students' "funds of knowledge" at home and in their communities through home visits and mapping of these important resources.

- González, N., Moll, L. C., & Amanti, C. (Eds.). (2006). *Funds of knowledge: Theorizing practices in households, communities, and classrooms.* Routledge.

Important facts about multilingual students:

- Go to https://www.colorincolorado.org and search for Fast Facts about ELLs.
- The Department of Education also publishes facts about multilingual student who receive ELD services: https://www2.ed.gov/datastory/el-characteristics/index.html#one

CHAPTER 2

Creating a Welcoming Classroom:

The Colorín Colorado website has an essay with embedded videos demonstrating how to create a welcoming atmosphere for multilingual students:

- https://www.colorincolorado.org/article/how-create-welcoming-classroom-environment

Restorative Justice Circles:

Helpful guides for using restorative justice circles and role play scenarios:

- Go to http://restorativejustice.org/. To explore the resources for those specific to schools, search the RJE Archive with the keyword "school."
- University of Michigan's Office of Student Conflict Resolution at https://oscr.umich.edu/RestorativeJustice
- International Institute for Restorative Practices at https://www.iirp.edu

Translanguaging:

The City University of New York–New York State Initiative on Emergent Bilinguals (CUNY-NYSIEB) YouTube Channel has a wealth of information about translanguaging, including lesson videos and teacher interviews. One of the playlists is aptly titled *Teaching Bilinguals (Even if You're Not One)*.

- Go to https://www.youtube.com/, search for "CUNY-NYSIEB" to access the channel, and search among the videos with the key word "translanguaging"

Ofelia García and Li Wei have authored an excellent book on translanguaging.

- García, O., & Wei, L. (2014). *Translanguaging: Language, bilingualism and education.* Palgrave McMillan.

CHAPTER 3

Comprehensible input:

This blog provides helpful information about comprehensible input and why it is important for language learning. Check out the video of Krashen demonstrating a lesson with and without comprehensible input.

- https://www.leonardoenglish.com/blog/comprehensible-input

Scaffolding:

This posting gives examples of scaffolding and helps distinguish between scaffolding and differentiation:

- https://www.edutopia.org/blog/scaffolding-lessons-six-strategies -rebecca-alber

Differentiation:

There are many different helpful examples and explanations of differentiation online. Try looking some up to see what provides you with additional support regarding how to differentiate in your teaching.

- Here is an example about student choice boards: https://theart ofeducation.edu/2012/07/11/how-to-use-choice-boards-to -differentiate-learning

Content and language objectives:

This example provides helpful details about writing content and language objectives:

- https://www.colorincolorado.org/article/language-objectives-key
  -effective-content-area-instruction-english-learners

You can also find great explanations from Twitter user Dr. José Medina about a number of topics related to teaching multilingual students, including writing objectives.

- His Twitter handle is @JoseMedinaJr89

There are also many websites that provide helpful ideas for linking objectives to higher order skills (Bloom's taxonomy).

- https://tips.uark.edu/using-blooms-taxonomy

CHAPTER 4

Vocabulary development in English:

It is useful to know the meaning and use of common root words in English, as well as the meanings of common prefixes and suffixes.

- One useful resource for these common words and word parts can be found here: https://www.readingrockets.org/article/root-words-roots
  -and-affixes

Vocabulary development and home language knowledge:

Google Translate will define words and provide a translation in other languages, and it offers an opportunity to play the word spoken aloud. This is helpful if you want to provide a spoken translation of vocabulary in students' home languages but do not speak that language yourself.

- translate.google.com

Colorín Colorado's articles about teaching vocabulary to multilingual students

An article about vocabulary development in general:

- https://www.colorincolorado.org/article/vocabulary-development

An article about the components of vocabulary instruction:

- https://www.colorincolorado.org/article/components-effective
  -vocabulary-instruction

An article about teaching vocabulary in grades 4–12:

- https://www.colorincolorado.org/article/tips-educators-ells-teaching
  -vocabulary-grades-4-12

Receptive and productive language skills:

Flipgrid is a resource that allows students to make a video recording of themselves speaking and then uploading it to be accessed later. You can examine their progress over time, help them get more comfortable with speaking without the pressure of an audience, listen to one another for comprehension, among many other uses.

- https://info.flipgrid.com

Listenwise is a resource that has a wide variety of listening activities to use with students, organized by content area and grade level. It includes short stories and podcasts, and students can change the speed of the delivery of the material.

- www.listenwise.com

Newsela offers many high-interest articles to support literacy development in different content areas, and allows teachers to choose reading materials aligned with particular standards.

- www.newsela.com

Valentina Gonzalez has a helpful blog called Serving Multilingual Learners of All Ages. Her post titled *Serving ELLs through reading and writing workshops* demonstrates how to address both receptive and productive language skills in the same lesson.

- https://www.valentinaesl.com/blog/serving-ells-through-reading
  -writing-workshop

CHAPTER 5

Informal and performance-based assessments:

Colorín Colorado has an article on using informal assessments, including performance-based assessments and portfolios, with multilingual students.

- https://www.colorincolorado.org/article/using-informal-assessments -english-language-learners

Rubrics:

Indiana University and Purdue University have a helpful guide for creating great rubrics. Go to ctl.iupui.edu and search for "Creating and Using Rubrics" or go to the web address.

- https://ctl.iupui.edu/Resources/Assessing-Student-Learning/Creating- and-Using-Rubrics

WIDA Access:

Elementary school ESOL specialist Kelsey Davis has a YouTube channel that includes videos on the WIDA Access test, using WIDA scores in the mainstream classrooms, and creating authentic assessments for multilingual students.

- https://www.youtube.com/channel/UCqmO5VPSP9mLtRXdZFyyZJA

Accommodations:

Colorín Colorado has a video in which language expert Lynn Shafer Willner describes accommodations for multilingual students.

- https://www.colorincolorado.org/video/assessment-accommodations-ells

CHAPTER 6

Collaborating with Colleagues:

Check out the video on "Learning Walks" to see how colleagues observe each others' classrooms and offer important feedback to each other.

- https://www.edutopia.org/article/3-ways-unlock-wisdom-colleagues

Relationship-Building:

This resource offers examples of ways that you can connect and engage with the families of your multilingual students.

- https://www.colorincolorado.org/article/connecting-ell-families-strategies-success

Engaging in Self-Care:

This website provides resources for teachers to engage in self-care and to bring mindfulness into the classroom. Be sure to view the videos and lesson resources that you can share with your students.

- https://www.mindfulschools.org

Advocacy:

This guide from Colorín Colorado provides an overview on how to engage in advocacy for multilingual students and their families.

- https://www.colorincolorado.org/sites/default/files/ELL_Advocacy Guide2015.pdf

Diane Staehr-Fenner has written a helpful book about advocacy: Staehr-Fenner, D. (2013). *Advocating for English learners.* Corwin Press.

References

Aguirre-Munoz, Z., & Boscardin, C. K. (2008). Opportunity to learn and English learner achievement: Is increased content exposure beneficial? *Journal of Latinos & Education, 7*(3), 86–205.

Anzaldúa, G. (1987). *Borderland/La Frontera: The new mestiza*. Spinsters/Aunt Lute Book Co.

Athanases, S. Z., & De Oliveira, L. C. (2008). Advocacy for equity in classrooms and beyond: New teachers' challenges and responses. *Teachers College Record, 110*(1), 64–104.

Au, K.H.P. (1980). Participation structures in a reading lesson with Hawaiian children: Analysis of a culturally appropriate instructional event. *Anthropology & Education Quarterly, 11*(2), 91–115.

Auerbach, S. (Ed.) (2012). *School leadership for authentic family and community partnerships*. Routledge.

August, D. E., & Shanahan, T. E. (2006). *Developing literacy in second-language learners: Report of the National Literacy Panel on language-minority children and youth*. Lawrence Erlbaum Associates Publishers.

Baecher, L., Artigliere, M., Patterson, D. K., & Spatzer, A. (2012). Differentiated instruction for English language learners as "variations on a theme": Teachers can differentiate instruction to support English language learners. *Middle School Journal, 43*(3), 14–21.

Baecher, L., Farnsworth, T., & Ediger, A. (2014). The challenges of planning language objectives in content-based ESL instruction. *Language Teaching Research, 18*(1), 118–136.

Bailey, A. L., & Carroll, P. E. (2015). Assessment of English language learners in the era of new academic content standards. *Review of Research in Education, 39*(1), 253–294.

Baker, C., & Wright, W. E. (2017). *Foundations of bilingual education and bilingualism* (6th ed.). Multilingual Matters.

Barnes, N., Fives, H., & Dacey, C. M. (2015). Teachers' beliefs about assessment. In H. Fives & M. G. Gill (Eds.), *International handbook of research on teacher beliefs* (pp. 284–300). Routledge.

Barone, J., Khairallah, P., & Gabriel, R. (2020). Running records revisited: A tool for efficiency and focus. *The Reading Teacher, 73*(4), 525–530.

Bartolomé, L. (1994). Beyond the methods fetish: Toward a humanizing pedagogy. *Harvard Educational Review, 64*(2), 173–195.

Bartolomé, L. I. (2008). Authentic cariño and respect in minority education: The political and ideological dimensions of love. *The International Journal of Critical Pedagogy, 1*(1), 1–17.

Beck, I. L., McKeown, M. G., & Kucan, L. (2013). *Bringing words to life: Robust vocabulary instruction.* Guilford Press.

Beck, I. L., McKeown, M. G., & Kucan, L. (2005). Choosing words to teach. In E. Hiebert & M. Kamil (Eds.) *Teaching and learning vocabulary: Bringing research to practice* (pp. 209–222). Taylor & Francis.

Bialystok, E. (2011). Reshaping the mind: The benefits of bilingualism. *Canadian Journal of Experimental Psychology, 65*(4), 229–235.

Black, P., & Wiliam, D. (2010). Inside the black box: Raising standards through classroom assessment. *Phi Delta Kappan, 92*(1), 81–90.

Box, C. (2019). *Formative assessment in United States classrooms.* Palgrave Macmillan.

Brisk, M. E. (2015). *Engaging students in academic literacies: Genre-based pedagogy for K–5 classrooms.* Routledge.

Brown, C. L., & Endo, R. (2017). The challenges of differentiating instruction for ELLs. *Teacher Education and Practice, 30*(3), 372–385.

Bunch, G. C., Kibler, A. K., & Pimentel, S. (2012). Realizing opportunities for English learners in the Common Core English language arts and disciplinary literacy standards. Paper presented at the 2013 Annual Meeting of the American Educational Research Association, May 1, 2013, San Francisco. https://ell.stanford.edu/sites/default/files/events/Bunch-Kibler-Pimentel_AERA_2013-04-08.pdf

Caldera, A., Whitaker, M. C., & Conrad Popova, D. A. (2020). Classroom management in urban schools: Proposing a course framework. *Teaching Education, 31*(3), 343–361.

Carter Andrews, D. J., & Castillo, B. (2016). Humanizing pedagogy for examinations of race and culture in teacher education. In F. Tuitt, C. Haynes, & S. Stewart (Eds.), *Race, equity and higher education: The continued search for critical and inclusive pedagogies around the globe* (pp. 112–130). Stylus.

Carter, P. L., & Welner, K. G. (Eds.). (2013). *Closing the opportunity gap: What America must do to give every child an even chance.* Oxford University Press.

CASEL (2021). *CASEL's SEL framework: What are the core competence areas and where are they promoted?* https://casel.org/sel-framework

Castro-Olivo, S. M. (2014). Promoting social-emotional learning in adolescent Latino ELLs: A study of the culturally adapted Strong Teens program. *School Psychology Quarterly, 29*(4), 567–577.

Castro-Olivo, S. M., Preciado, J. A., Sanford, A. K., & Perry, V. (2011). The academic and social-emotional needs of secondary Latino English learners: Implications for screening, identification, and instructional planning. *Exceptionality, 19*(3), 160–174.

Chamberlain, S. P. (2005). Recognizing and responding to cultural differences in the education of culturally and linguistically diverse learners. *Intervention in School and Clinic, 40*(4), 195–211.

Collier, V. P. (1995). *Promoting academic success for ESL students: Understanding second language acquisition for school.* New Jersey Teachers of English to Speakers of Other Languages–Bilingual Educators.

Cornelius-White, J. (2007). Learner-centered teacher student relationships are effective: A meta-analysis. *Review of Educational Research, 77*(1), 113–143.

Counts, J., Katsiyannis, A., & Whitford, D. K. (2018). Culturally and linguistically diverse learners in special education: English learners. *NASSP Bulletin, 102*(1), 5–21.

Crandall, J., Stein, H., & Nelson, J. (2012). What kinds of knowledge and skills do general education teachers, English as a second language teachers, bilingual teachers, and support staff need to implement an effective program for English language learners? In E. Hamayan & R. Freeman Field (Eds.), *English language learners at school: A guide for administrators.* Caslon Publishing.

Crosby, S. D., Howell, P., & Thomas, S. (2018). Social justice education through trauma-informed teaching. *Middle School Journal, 49*(4), 15–23.

Dabach, D. B. (2014). "I am not a shelter!": Stigma and social boundaries in teachers' accounts of students' experience in separate "sheltered" English learner class-rooms. *Journal of Education for Students Placed at Risk, 19*(2), 98–124.

Daniels, J. R., & Varghese, M. (2020). Troubling practice: Exploring the relationship between Whiteness and practice-based teacher education in considering a racio-linguicized teacher subjectivity. *Educational Researcher, 49*(1), 56–63.

DeCapua, A., & Marshall, H. W. (2011). *Breaking new ground: Teaching students with limited or interrupted formal education in U.S. secondary schools.* University of Michigan Press.

DelliCarpini, M. (2008). Teacher collaboration for ESL/EFL academic success. *Internet TESL Journal, 14*(8). Retrieved from http://iteslj.org/Techniques/DelliCarpini -TeacherCollaboration.html

DelliCarpini, M. (2009). Success with ELLs: Authentic assessment for ELLs in the ELA classroom. *The English Journal, 98*(5), 116–119.

Delpit, L. (1988). The silenced dialogue: Power and pedagogy in educating other people's children. *Harvard Educational Review, 58*(3), 280–299.

Department of Homeland Security. (n.d.) *Yearbook of immigration statistics.* https:// www.dhs.gov/immigration-statistics/yearbook

Derewianka, B., & Jones, P. (2016). *Teaching language in context* (2nd ed.). Oxford University Press.

Dove, M., & Honigsfeld, A. (2010). ESL coteaching and collaboration: Opportuni-ties to develop teacher leadership and enhance student learning. *TESOL Journal, 1*(1), 3–22.

Dubetz, N. E., & de Jong, E. J. (2011). Teacher advocacy in bilingual programs. *Bilingual Research Journal, 38*(3), 248–262.

Dutro, E., & Cartun, A. (2016). Cut to the core practices: Toward visceral disruptions of binaries in PRACTICE-based teacher education. *Teaching and Teacher Education, 58*(1), 119–128.

Echevarría, J., Short, D., & Powers, K. (2008). Making content comprehensible for non-native speakers of English: The SIOP Model. *The International Journal of Learning, 14*(11), 41–50.

Fairbairn, S., & Jones-Vo, S. (2010). *Differentiating instruction and assessment for English language learners: A guide for K–12 teachers.* Caslon Publishing.

Fang, Z., & Coatoam, S. (2013). Disciplinary literacy: What you want to know about it. *Journal of Adolescent & Adult Literacy, 56*(8), 627–632.

Flores, N., & Rosa, J. (2015). Undoing appropriateness: Raciolinguistic ideologies and language diversity in education. *Harvard Educational Review, 85*(2), 149–171.

Fox, R., Corretjer, O., & Webb, K. (2019). Benefits of foreign language learning and bilingualism: An analysis of published empirical research 2012–2019. *Foreign Language Annals, 52*(4), 699–726.

Fredricks, D. E., & Peercy, M. M. (2020). Youth perspectives on humanizing core practices. In L. Cardozo-Gaibisso & M. V. Dominguez (Eds.), *Handbook of research on advancing language equity practices within immigrant communities* (pp. 107–128). IGI Global.

García, O., & Kleifgen, J. A. (2010). *Educating emergent bilinguals: Policies, programs, and practices for English language learners.* Teachers College Press.

García, O., & Lin, A. M. (2017). Translanguaging in bilingual education. In O. García, A. M. Lin, & S. May (Eds.), *Bilingual and multilingual education* (pp. 117–130). Springer.

Gay, G. (2006). Connections between classroom management and culturally responsive teaching. In C. M. Evertson & C. S. Weinstein (Eds.), *Handbook of classroom management: Research, practice, and contemporary issues,* (pp. 343–370). Routledge.

Gee, J. P. (2015). Discourse, small d, big D. In K. Tracy, C. Ilie, & T. Sandel (Eds.), *The international encyclopedia of language and social interaction,* (vol. 3, pp. 1–5). Blackwell. https://academic.jamespaulgee.com/pubs/big-d-small-d/

Gibbons, P. (2003). Mediating language learning: Teacher interactions with ESL students in a content-based classroom. *TESOL Quarterly, 37*(2), 247–273.

Gibbons, P. (2015). *Scaffolding language, scaffolding learning: Teaching English language learners in the mainstream classroom* (2nd ed.). Heinemann.

Glisan, E. W., & Donato, R. (2017). *Enacting the work of language instruction: High-leverage teaching practices.* American Council on the Teaching of Foreign Languages.

Goldenberg, C. (2013). Unlocking the research on English Learners: What we know—and don't yet know—about effective instruction. *American Educator, 37*(2), 4–11, 38.

Grabe, M. (2009). *Reading in a second language: Moving from theory to practice.* Cambridge University Press.

Graves, M. F. (2006). *Vocabulary learning and instruction.* Teachers College Press.

Grossman, P. (2018). *Teaching core practices in teacher education.* Harvard Education Press.

Hakuta, K. (2014). Assessment of content and language in light of the new standards: Challenges and opportunities for English language learners. *The Journal of Negro Education, 83*(4), 433–441.

Hamayan, E., & Field, R. F. (2012). *English learners at school: A guide for administrators.* Caslon Publishing.

Hamre, B. K., & Pianta, R. C. (2006). Student–teacher relationships. In G. G. Bear & K. M. Minke (Eds.), *Children's needs III: Development, prevention, and intervention* (pp. 59–71). National Association of School Psychologists.

Haneda, M. (2014). From academic language to academic communication: Building on English learners' resources. *Linguistics and Education, 26*(1), 126–135.

Hatch, E. (1983). Simplified input and second language acquisition. In R. W. Andersen (Ed.), *Pidginization and creolization as language acquisition* (pp. 64–86). Newbury House.

Haycock, K. (2001). Closing the achievement gap. *Educational Leadership, 58*(6), 6–11.

Heath, S. B. (1983). *Ways with words.* Cambridge University Press.

Hernandez, R. D. (1994). Reducing bias in the assessment of culturally and linguistically diverse populations. *The Journal of Educational Issues of Language Minority Students, 14*(3), 269–300.

Hill, J., & Miller, K. B. (2013). *Classroom instruction that works with English language learners.* (2nd ed.). ASCD.

Hood, B. (2018). *Exploring equity issues: Bio-social-emotional needs of immigrant students, with a focus on Central Americans.* Center for Education Equity, Mid-Atlantic Equity Consortium.

Hopewell, S. (2011). Leveraging bilingualism to accelerate English reading comprehension. *International Journal of Bilingual Education and Bilingualism, 14*(5), 603–620.

Howard, T. C. (2017). Relationships & learning: Keys to academic success. *TeachingWorks, Working Papers.*

Hyland, K. (2007). Genre pedagogy: Language, literacy and L2 writing instruction. *Journal of Second Language Writing, 16*(3), 148–164.

Ishimaru, A. M. (2020). *Just schools: Building equitable collaborations with families and communities.* Teachers College Press.

Jennings, P. A. (2015). *Mindfulness for teachers.* Norton.

Jennings, P. A., Frank, J. L., Snowberg, K. E., Coccia, M. A., & Greenberg, M. E. (2013). Improving classroom learning environments by Cultivating Awareness and Resilience in Education (CARE): Results of a randomized controlled trial. *School of Psychology Quarterly, 28*(4), 374–390.

Jennings, P. A., & Greenberg, M. T. (2009). The prosocial classroom: Teacher social and emotional competence in relation to student and classroom outcomes. *Review of Educational Research, 79*(1), 491–525.

Jiménez, R. T., García, G. E., & Pearson, P. D. (1996). The reading strategies of bilingual Latina/o students who are successful English readers: Opportunities and obstacles. *Reading Research Quarterly, 31*(1), 90–112.

Kinloch, V. (2015). Critically conscious teaching and instructional leadership as projects in humanization. *Education Review 4*(3), 29–35.

Kinloch, V. (2018). *Necessary disruptions: Examining justice, engagement, and humanizing approaches to teaching and teacher education.* Retrieved from https://www.teachingworks.org/images/files/TeachingWorks_Kinloch.pdf

Kinsella, K. (2005). Preparing for effective vocabulary instruction. *Aiming High.* Sonoma County Office of Education. Retrieved from http://www.scoe.org/docs/ah/AH_kinsella1.pdf

Krashen, S. (1985). *The input hypothesis: Issues and implications.* Longman.

Ladson-Billings, G. (1995). But that's just good teaching! The case for culturally relevant pedagogy. *Theory into Practice, 34*(3), 159–165.

Ladson-Billings, G. (2006). From the achievement gap to the education debt: Understanding achievement in U.S. schools. *Educational Researcher, 35*(7), 3–12.

Law, F., Mahr, T., Schneeberg, A., & Edwards, J. (2017). Vocabulary size and auditory word recognition in preschool children. *Applied Psycholinguistics, 38*(1), 89–125.

Lee, J. F., & VanPatten, B. (2003). *Making communicative language teaching happen* (2nd ed.). McGraw-Hill.

Lehr, F., Osborn, J., & Hiebert, E. (2005). *A focus on comprehension.* Research-based practices in early reading series. Pacific Resources for Education and Learning.

Lenski, S. D., Crawford, K., Crumpler, T., & Stallworth, C. (2005). Preparing preservice teachers in a diverse world. *Action in Teacher Education, 27*(3), 3–12.

Liu, D. (2015). A critical review of Krashen's input hypothesis: Three major arguments. *Journal of Education and Human Development, 4*(4), 139–146.

Long, M. H. (1983). Native speaker/non-native speaker conversation and the negotiation of comprehensible input. *Applied Linguistics, 4*(2), 126–141.

Lucas, T., Villegas, A. M., & Freedson-Gonzalez, M. (2008). Linguistically responsive teacher education: Preparing classroom teachers to teach English language learners. *Journal of Teacher Education, 59*(4), 361–373.

Lyster, R. (2007). *Learning and teaching languages through content: A counterbalanced approach.* John Benjamins.

MacGillivray, L., & Rueda, R. (2003). *Listening to inner city teachers of English language learners: Differentiating literacy instruction.* ED 479984.

Mansfield, K. C., Rainbolt, S., & Fowler, E. (2018). Implementing restorative justice as a step toward racial equity in school discipline. *Teachers College Record, 120*(14), 1–24.

Martin-Beltrán, M., & Peercy, M. M. (2012). How can ESOL and mainstream teachers make the best of a standards-based curriculum in order to collaborate? *TESOL Journal, 3*(3), 425–444.

Maybin, J., Mercer, N., & Stierer, B. (1992). "Scaffolding" learning in the classroom. In K. Norman (Ed.), *Thinking voices: The work of the national curriculum project* (pp. 165–195). Hodder & Stoughton.

McDonald, M., Kazemi, E., & Kavanagh, S. S. (2013). Core practices and pedagogies of teacher education: A call for a common language and collective activity. *Journal of Teacher Education, 64*(5), 378–386.

McIntyre, T., Barowsky, E. I., & Tong, V. (2011). The psychological, behavioral, and educational impact of immigration: Helping recent immigrant students to succeed in North American schools. *Journal of the American Academy of Special Education Professionals,* Fall, 4–21.

Menken, K., & Kleyn, T. (2009). The difficult road for long-term English learners. *Educational Leadership, 66*(7), 26–29.

Mercuri, S. P. (2012). Understanding the interconnectedness between language choices, cultural identity construction and school practices in the life of a Latina educator. *Gist: Education and Learning Research Journal, 6,* 12–43.

Meyers, M., & Rodriguez, R. C. (2012). How do we integrate parents of English language learners and community members into our program/school? In E. Hamayan & R. Freeman Field (Eds.), *English language learners at school: A guide for administrators.* Caslon Publishing.

Michaels, S. (1981). "Sharing time": Children's narrative styles and differential access to literacy. *Language in Society, 10*(3), 423–442.

Milner, H. R., Cunningham, H. B., Delale-O'Connor, L., & Kestenberg, E. G. (2018). *"These kids are out of control": Why we must reimagine "classroom management" for equity.* Corwin Press.

Milner, H. R., & Tenore, F. B. (2010). Classroom management in diverse classrooms. *Urban Education, 45*(5), 560–603.

Mirsky, L. (2011). Restorative practices: Giving everyone a voice to create safer saner school communities. *Prevention Researcher, 18*(5), 3–6.

Nagy, W. E., & Scott J. A. (2000). Vocabulary processes. In M. Kamil, P. Mosenthal, P. D. Pearson, & R. Barr (Eds.), *Handbook of Reading Research, Volume III,* (pp. 269–284). Lawrence Erlbaum Associates.

National Clearinghouse for English Language Acquisition. (n.d.). www.ncela.ed.gov.

Newbould, S. (2018). Classroom Contract. *English Teaching Forum, 56*(4), 37–39.

Niehaus, K., & Adelson, J. L. (2014). School support, parental involvement, and academic and social-emotional outcomes for English language learners. *American Educational Research Journal, 51*(4), 810–844.

Olsen, L. (2012). *Secondary school courses designed to address the language needs and academic gaps of long term English learners.* Californians Together.

Orosco, M. J., & O'Connor, R. (2014). Culturally responsive instruction for English language learners with learning disabilities. *Journal of Learning Disabilities, 47*(6), 515–531.

Pacheco, M. B., & Miller, M. E. (2016). Making meaning through translanguaging in the literacy classroom. *The Reading Teacher, 69*(5), 533–537.

Paris, D., & Alim, H. S. (Eds.). (2017). *Culturally sustaining pedagogies: Teaching and learning for justice in a changing world.* Teachers College Press.

Peercy, M. M., & Martin-Beltrán, M. (2011). Envisioning collaboration: Including ESOL students *and* teachers in the mainstream classroom. *International Journal of Inclusive Education, 16*(7), 657–673.

Peercy, M. M., Tigert, J., Feagin, K., Kidwell, T., Fredricks, D., Lawyer, M., Bitter, M., Canales, N., & Mallory, A. (2019a). "I need to take care of myself.": The case of self-care as a core practice for teaching. In C. R. Rinke & L. Mawhinney (Eds.), *Opportunities and challenges in teacher recruitment and retention: Teacher voices across the pipeline* (pp. 303–325). Information Age Publishing.

Peercy, M. M., Varghese, M., & Dubetz, N. (2019b). Critically examining practice-based teacher education for teachers of language minoritized youth. *TESOL Quarterly, 53*(4), 1174–1185.

Philip, T., Souto-Manning, M., Anderson, L., Horn, I., Andrews, D. J. C., Stillman, J., & Varghese, M. (2019). Making justice peripheral by constructing practice as "core": How the increasing prominence of core practices challenges teacher education. *Journal of Teacher Education, 70*(3), 251–264.

Pierce, L. V. (2002). Performance-based assessment: Promoting achievement for English language learners. *ERIC/CLL News Bulletin, 26*(1), 1–3.

Rafferty, L. A. (2007). Teaching strategies: "They just won't listen to me": A teacher's guide to positive behavioral interventions. *Childhood Education, 84*(2), 102–104.

Ramirez, P. C., Faltis, C. J., & de Jong, E. J. (2017). Critical teacher education: A multilens framework for transformation. In P. C. Ramírez, C. J. Faltis, & E. J. de Jong (Eds.), *Learning from Emergent Bilingual Latinx Learners in K–12* (pp. 3–14). Routledge.

Rasooli, A., Zandi, H., & DeLuca, C. (2018). Re-conceptualizing classroom assessment fairness: A systematic meta-ethnography of assessment literature and beyond. *Studies in Educational Evaluation, 56*, 164–181.

Reyes, R. (2017). Humanization through presence, proximity, and problematizing Latino/a ELLs in teacher education. In P. C. Ramírez, C. J. Faltis, & E. J. de Jong (Eds.), *Learning from Emergent Bilingual Latinx Learners in K–12* (pp. 103–121). Routledge.

Roos, P. D. (2020). *Putting my mind and heart to educational equity: Memoirs of an advocate.* Center for Applied Linguistics.

Rose, D., & Martin, J. R. (2012). *Learning to write, reading to learn: Genre, knowledge and pedagogy in the Sydney School.* Equinox.

Ross, D. D., Bondy, E., Bondy, E., & Hambacher, E. (2008). Promoting academic engagement through insistence: Being a warm demander. *Childhood Education*, *84*(3), 142–146.

Saito, K., & Akiyama, Y. (2018). Effects of video-based interaction on the development of second language listening comprehension ability: A longitudinal study. *TESOL Quarterly*, *52*(1), 163–176.

Salazar, M. del C. (2010). Pedagogical stances of high school ESL teachers: Huelgas in high school ESL classrooms. *Bilingual Research Journal*, *33*(1), 111–124.

Salazar, M. del C. (2013). A humanizing pedagogy: Reinventing the principles and practice of education as a journey toward liberation. *Review of Research in Education*, *37*(1), 121–148.

Santamaría, L. J. (2009). Culturally responsive differentiated instruction: Narrowing gaps between best pedagogical practices benefiting all learners. *Teachers College Record*, *111*(1), 214–247.

Santiago-Negrón, N. (2012). How can we move from advocacy for English language learners to activism by English language learners and their families? In E. Hamayan & R. Freeman Field, (Eds.), *English language learners at school: A guide for administrators*. Caslon Publishing.

Saunders, W. M., & O'Brien, G. (2006). Oral language. In F. Genesee, K. Lindholm-Leary, D. Christian, W. M. Saunders, & D. Christian (Eds.), *Educating English language learners: A synthesis of research evidence*, (14–63). Cambridge University Press.

Schmitt, N., Jiang, X., & Grabe, W. (2011). The percentage of words known in a text and reading comprehension. *The Modern Language Journal*, *95*(1), 26–43.

Scullin, B. L., & Baron, H. L. (2013). Using freewriting notebooks to reduce writing anxiety for English language learners. *California Reader*, *47*(1).

Siegel, M. A. (2014). Developing preservice teachers' expertise in equitable assessment for English learners. *Journal of Science Teacher Education*, *25*(3), 289–308.

Siwatu, K. O., Putman, S. M., Starker-Glass, T. V., & Lewis, C. W. (2017). The culturally responsive classroom management self-efficacy scale: Development and initial validation. *Urban Education*, *52*(7), 862–888.

Sleeter, C., & Zavala, M. (2020). *Transformative ethnic studies in schools: Curriculum, pedagogy, and research*. Teachers College Press.

Snow, C. E., Griffin, P. E., & Burns, M. (2005). *Knowledge to support the teaching of reading: Preparing teachers for a changing world*. Jossey-Bass.

Souto-Manning, M. (2010). *Freire, teaching, and learning: Culture circles across contexts*. Peter Lang.

Spilt, J. L., Koomen, H. M., & Thijs, J. T. (2011). Teacher wellbeing: The importance of teacher–student relationships. *Educational Psychology Review*, *23*(4), 457–477.

Swain, M. (1985). Communicative competence: Some roles of comprehensible input and comprehensible output in its development. In S. Gass & C. Madden (Eds.), *Input in second language acquisition* (pp. 235–256). Newbury House.

TeachingWorks. (2021). *High leverage practices*. Retrieved from http://www.teachingworks.org/work-of-teaching/high-leverage-practices.

Teemant, A. (2014). A mixed methods investigation of instructional coaching for teachers of diverse learners. *Urban Education*, *49*(5), 574–604.

Thomas, W. P., & V. P. Collier. (1997). *School effectiveness for language minority students*. National Clearinghouse for Bilingual Education.

Thompson, J. (2018). *The first-year teacher's survival guide: Ready-to-use strategies, tools, & activities for meeting the challenges of each school day* (4th ed.). John Wiley & Sons, Inc.

Tienda, M., & Haskins, R. (2011). Immigrant children: Introducing the issue. *The Future of Children, 21*(1), 3–18.

Tomlinson, C. A. (2003). *Fulfilling the promise of the differentiated classroom: Strategies and tools for responsive teaching.* ASCD.

Tomlinson, C. A. (2008). The goals of differentiation. *Educational Leadership, 66*(3), 26–30.

Tomlinson, C. A. (2014). *The differentiated classroom: Responding to the needs of all learners* (2nd ed.). ASCD.

Turkan, S., & Buzick, H. M. (2016). Complexities and issues to consider in the evaluation of content teachers of English language learners. *Urban Education, 51*(2), 221–248.

Turkan, S., De Oliveira, L. C., Lee, O., & Phelps, G. 2014. Proposing a knowledge base for teaching academic content to English language learners: Disciplinary linguistic knowledge. *Teachers College Record, 116*(4), 1–30.

Uchihara, T., Webb, S., & Yanagisawa, A. (2019). The effects of repetition on incidental vocabulary learning: A meta-analysis of correlational studies. *Language Learning, 69*(3), 559–599.

Vadasy, P. F., & Nelson, J. R. (2012). *Vocabulary instruction for struggling students.* Guilford Press.

Valdés, G., Kibler, A., & Philipose, S. (2004). What does research show about the benefits of language learning? Retrieved from https://www.actfl.org/assessment-research-and-development/what-the-research-shows

Vygotsky, L. S. (1962). *Thought and language.* MIT Press.

Vygotsky, L. S. (1978). *Mind in society: The development of higher psychological processes* (M. Cole, V. John-Steiner, S. Scribner & E. Souberman, Eds.). Harvard University Press.

Walqui, A., & Heritage, M. (2018). Meaningful classroom talk: Supporting English learners' oral language development. *American Educator, 42*(3), 18–39.

WestEd. (2016). *Long-term English learner students: Spotlight on an overlooked population.* https://www.wested.org/wp-content/uploads/2016/11/LTEL-factsheet.pdf

Wiggins, G., & McTighe, J. (2005). *Understanding by design.* ASCD.

Windschitl, M., Thompson, J., Braaten, M., & Stroupe, D. (2012). Proposing a core set of instructional practices and tools for teachers of science. *Science Education, 96*(5), 878–903.

Wong, S., & Grant, R. (2007). Academic achievement and social identity among bilingual students in the U.S. In J. Cummins & C. Davison (Eds.), *International handbook of English language teaching* (pp. 681–691). Springer.

Wright, W. (2015). *Foundations for teaching English language learners: Research, theory, policy, and practice.* Caslon Publishing.

Wright, W. (2012). What are some concrete strategies that administrators and teachers can use to guide advocacy for English language learners on the local level? In E. Hamayan & R. Freeman Field (Eds.), *English language learners at school: A guide for administrators.* Caslon Publishing.

Wubbels, T., & Brekelmans, M. (2005). Two decades of research on teacher–student relationships in class. *International Journal of Educational Research, 43*(1–2), 6–24.

Xu, Y., & Brown, G. T. (2016). Teacher assessment literacy in practice: A reconceptualization. *Teaching and Teacher Education, 58*, 149–162.

Young, E. (2010). Challenges to conceptualizing and actualizing culturally relevant pedagogy: How viable is the theory in classroom practice? *Journal of Teacher Education, 61*(3), 248–260.

Zong, J., & Batalova, J. (2015). *The limited English proficient population in the United States.* Migration Policy Institute. http://www.migrationpolicy.org/article/limited -english-proficient-population-united-states#Age,%20Race,%20and%20 Ethnicity

Index

Academic rigor, humanizing pedagogy and, 6
Adelson, J. L., 34
Administrators, humanizing practice
    challenges and, 135–136
Advocacy, engaging in, 101–104.
    See also Relationship-building
    (core practice)
Affective language, 35
Aguirre-Munoz, Z., 44
Akiyama, Y., 44
Alim, H. S., 28, 30
Anderson, L., 4
Andrea (elementary ESOL teacher),
    classroom practice examples
  building positive learning environment,
    37–39
  relationship-building and advocacy,
    106–107
Andrew (elementary ESOL teacher), 43
  assessment classroom practice example,
    85–89
Andrews, D. J. C., 4
Anzaldúa, G., 13
Artigliere, M., 44, 47–48
Assessment (core practice), viii, 25, 131–132
  classroom examples, 85–92
  dimensions of, 77–78
  teaching techniques/methods/resources,
    92–93, 145
  types of, 76–77
Athanases, S. Z., 13
Au, K., 18
Auerbach, S., 99
August, D. E., 15
Authentic assessment, 80–81, 84, 92

Baecher, L., 44, 47–48, 51
Bailey, A. L., 77
Baker, C., 64
Barnes, N., 81
Baron, H. L., 66

Barone, J., 78
Barowsky, E. I., 34
Bartolomé, L.I., 5, 6, 29, 30, 78
Batalova, J., 16
Beck, I. L., 62, 63
Behavior, multi-tiered support for, 35–36
Bialystok, E., 65
Black, P., 76
Boscardin, C. K., 44
Box, C., 76
Braaten, M., 2
Brekelmans, M., 13
Brisk, M. E., 70
Brown, C. L., 44
Brown, G. T., 77
Bunch, G. C., viii, 61
Burns, M., 15
Buzick, H. M., 83

Caldera, A., 28, 29
Caring language, 35
Carroll, P. E., 77
Carter, P. L., 4
Carter Andrews, D. J., 5, 6, 33
Cartun, A., 4
CASEL, 34
Castillo, B., 5, 6, 33
Castro-Olivo, S. M., 28, 34
Chamberlain, S. P., 77
Chris (secondary ESOL teacher), 27, 94
  building positive learning environment
    example, 39–41
Classroom teachers
  autonomy of, 127–128
  comprehensive input examples, 45
  content and language objectives, 52–53
  pedagogical practice examples of.
    See individually named teachers
  professional development supporting,
    132–137, 145–146
  self-care for, 105–106, 145

Classroom teachers (*continued*)
  stakeholder communication/coordination
    and, 131
  time constraints and, 128–131
Coatoam, S., 61
Coccia, M. A., 105
Collaboration with colleagues, 96–98, 129
  teaching techniques/methods/resources,
    109–110, 145
Collaborative protocols, high school lesson
    example, 118–124
Collier, V. P., 64
Communication, stakeholder, 131
Community
  establishing bonds with, viii, 26
  student experiences of, 17–18, 25
Community Helpers (elementary classroom
    practice example), 111–118
Comprehensible input, 44–46, 142
  in content and language instruction, 59
  differentiation and, 48
Conrad Popova, D. A., 28, 29
Content
  differentiated instruction and, 48, 49–50
  engagement with, 33
Content and language instruction
    (core practice), viii
  classroom examples, 53–59
  dimensions of, 43–53
  integrated objectives for, 50–53, 60–61, 143
  teaching techniques/methods/resources,
    59–60, 143
Coordination, stakeholder, 131
Core practices. *See also individually named
    core practices*
  in elementary lesson plan example, 111–118
  in high school lesson plan example, 118–124
  identified, 2–3
  lesson analysis templates, 125–126
  purpose, 4
  reflective questions on, 138
  resources/assignments/activities, 139–140
Cornelius-White, J., 96
Corretjer, O., 64, 65
Counts, J., 77
Crandall, J., 98
Crawford, K., 4
Crosby, S. D., 34
Crumpler, T., 4
Culturally and linguistically responsive
    classroom
  content engagement strategies in, 33
  learning differences and, 32–33

teaching techniques/methods/resources,
    41, 142
  translanguaging in, 31–32
Culturally and linguistically responsive/
    sustaining pedagogy (CLRP), viii, 30–33
Cunningham, H. B., 30, 94, 99

Dabach, D. B., 17, 28
Dacey, C. M., 81
Daniels, J. R., 4
de Jong, E. J., 46, 102
De Oliveira, L. C., 13, 69
DeCapua, A., 29
DelliCarpini, M., 80, 96
Delpit, L., 28
DeLuca, C., 77
Department of Homeland Security, 16
Derewianka, B., 70
Development Reading Assessment (DRA), 83
Differentiating assessment, 50, 83–85
Differentiation/Differentiated instruction,
    47–50, 59, 142
  language development needs, 69–71, 144
Donato, R., 2
Dove, M., 98
Dubetz, N. E., 102
Dutro, E., 4

Echevarría, J., 51
Ediger, A., 51
Educational dignity, viii
Edwards, J., 62
Endo, R., 44
English language development (ELD) services,
    assessment and, 82, 83, 85
English language learners (ELLs).
    See Multilingual students
English language proficiency tests, 17, 82.
    See also WIDA ACCESS
  interpreting, 82–83
English learners (ELs). *See* Multilingual students
Equity, core practices and, 4
Erica (elementary ESOL teacher), 61
  Community Helpers lesson example,
    111–118
  content and language instruction example,
    55–57
  relationship-building and advocacy
    example, 108–109
Expectations, for students, 28–30, 41
  humanizing pedagogy and, 6
Extralinguistic support, comprehensible input
    and, 46

Fairbairn, S., 78, 84
Faltis, C. J., vii–viii, 46
Family, of multilingual students, 17, 18, 25
    involvement in SEL/outreach
        programs, 34
    meaningful connections with, 99
Fang, Z., 61
Farnsworth, T., 51
Feagin, K., viii
Field, R. F., 94, 103
Fives, H., 81
Flores, N., 26n1
Formative (informal) assessment, 76, 145
    designing and using, 78–81
Fowler, E., 36
Fox, R., 64, 65
Frank, J. L., 105
Fredricks, D. E., viii, 66
Freedson-Gonzalez, M., 30

Gabriel, R., 78
García, G. E., 65
García, O., vii, 7, 31
Gay, G., 30
Gee, J. P., 65
Gibbons, P., 2, 44
Glisan, E. W., 2
Goldenberg, C., 44
Grabe, M., 63
Grabe, W., 63
Grant, R., 61
Graves, M. F., 62
Greenberg, M. E., 105
Greenberg, M. T., 13
Griffin, P. E., 15
Grossman, P., 2

Hakuta, K., 79
Hamayan, E., 94, 103
Hamre, B. K., 12
Haneda, M., 28
Haskins, R., 34
Hatch, E., 45
Haycock, K., 47
Heath, S. B., 18
Heritage, M., 66
Hernandez, R. D., 77
Hiebert, E., 62
Hill, J., 51
Home experiences, of students, 17–18, 25
Home language, viii
    English language background/literacy and,
        13–16, 22–25

as resource for students, 64–66
Honigsfeld, A., 98
Hood, B., 34
Hopewell, S., 61
Horn, I., 4
Howard, T. C., 95
Howell, P., 34
Humanizing pedagogy/practice, 4–7.
    See also individually named core
        practices
    challenges and solutions in, 127–137
    culturally and linguistically/sustaining, viii,
        30–33
    developing/implementing, 127, 137
    elementary lesson example, 111–118
    in high school lesson example, 118–124
    lesson analysis templates, 124–125
    reflective questions on, 138
Hyland, K., 69

Immigrants, traumatic experiences among,
    34–35
Inferencing activity, 21
Instruction. See Content and language
    instruction (core practice);
    Differentiation/Differentiated
    instruction
Interests. See Student interests
Ishimaru, A. M., 99

Jacobson, R., vii
Jennings, P. A., 13, 95, 105
Jiang, X., 63
Jiménez, R. T., 65
Jones, P., 70
Jones-Vo, S., 78, 84
Justice, core practices and, 4

Katsiyannis, A., 77
Kavanagh, S. S., 2
Kazemi, E., 2
Kendall (elementary ESOL teacher),
        classroom practice examples
    knowing students, 19–20
    language and literacy development, 72–74
Kestenberg, E. G., 30, 94, 99
Khairallah, P., 78
Kibler, A. K., 61, 64
Kidwell, T., viii
Kinloch, V., 5
Kinsella, K., 62
Kleifgen, J. A., 7
Kleyn, T., 16, 17

Knowing students (core practice), viii, 12
  challenges of, 18–19
  classroom examples, 19–25
  dimensions of, 12–18
  teaching techniques/methods/resources,
      25–26, 140–141
Koomen, H. M., 13
Krashen, S., 44, 66
Kucan, L., 62, 63
KWL chart, use of, 79, 80

Ladson-Billings, G., 4, 30
Language and literacy development
    (core practice), viii
  classroom examples, 70–74
  complexity of, 61
  dimensions supporting, 62–70
  teaching techniques/methods/resources,
      74–75, 143–144
Language demands, defined/described, 51
Language instruction. *See* Content
    and language instruction
    (core practice)
Law, F., 62
Lawyer, M., viii
Learning environment. *See* Positive learning
    environment (core practice)
Learning profile, differentiation and, 49
Lee, J. F., 44
Lee, O., 69
Lehr, F., 62
Lenski, S. D., 4
Lesson analysis templates, 125–126
Lesson plans/planning
  analysis templates, 125–126
  collaborative, 118–124, 129
  elementary school example, 111–118
  high school example, 118–124
  scaffolding and, 47
Lewis, C. W., 6, 28
Lin, A. M., 31
Linguistically responsive classroom, viii,
    30–33. *See also* Culturally and
    linguistically responsive classroom
Lisa (secondary ESOL student teacher), 1
Literacy development. *See* Language and
    literacy development
Liu, D., 44
Long, M. H., 44
Long-term English learners (LTELs), 17
Lucas, T., 30
Lyster, R., 44

MacGillivray, L., 47
Mahr, T., 62
Mansfield, K. C., 36
Marshall, H. W., 29
Martin, J. R., 69
Martin-Beltrán, M., 94, 96
Maybin, J., 44
McDonald, M., 2
McIntyre, T., 34
McKeown, M. G., 62, 63
McTighe, J., 79
Melissa (secondary ESOL ELA teacher),
    classroom practice examples
  assessment, 89–92
  with collaborative protocols,
      118–124
  relationship-building and advocacy,
      107–108
Menken, K., 16, 17
Mercer, N., 44
Mercuri, S. P., 61
Michaels, S., 18
Miller, K. B., 51
Miller, M. E., 61
Milner, H. R., 28, 29, 30, 94, 99
Minoritized groups
  teacher understanding of, 17–18
  use of term, 26n1
Minoritized, use of term, 26n1
Mirsky, L., 36
Multi-tiered system of support (MTSS),
    35–36
Multilingual students, viii, 1. *See also* Student
    entries
  community experiences, 17–18, 25
  core practices for teaching, 2–3
  prior schooling experiences, 16–17, 19–20,
      25, 28–29
  traumatic experiences, 34–36
  use of term, 7

Nagy, W. E., 62
Nancy (secondary ESOL ELA teacher), 12
  content and language instruction practice
      example, 57–59
National Clearinghouse for English Language
    Acquisition, 1
Nelson, J. R., 15, 98
Newbould, S., 29
Niehaus, K., 34
Novice teachers, 1, 4, 6, 105. *See also* Erica
    (elementary ESOL teacher)

Objectives
    integrated, for content and language
        instruction, 50–53, 60–61
    lesson matched with assessment, 79–80
O'Brien, G., 66
O'Connor, L., 30, 94, 99
O'Connor, R., 32
Olsen, L., 28
Orosco, M. J., 32
Osborn, J., 62
Outlining organizer, 41

Pacheco, M. B., 61
Paris, D., 28, 30
Patterson, D. K., 44, 47–48
Pearson, P. D., 65
Pedagogy. *See* Humanizing pedagogy/practice
Peercy, M. M., viii, 66, 94, 96
Perry, V., 28, 34
Personal time, demands on, 130
Phelps, G., 69
Philip, T., 4
Philipose, S., 64
Pianta, R. C., 12
Pierce, L. V., 81
Pimentel, S., 61
Planning. *See* Lesson plans/planning
Plug-in lessons, 19, 26n2
Positive learning environment (core practice),
        building, viii, 27
    classroom examples, 36–40
    dimensions of, 27–36
    teaching techniques/methods/resources, 41,
        141–142
Power dynamics, humanizing pedagogy and,
        6–7
Powers, K., 51
Poza, L. E., viii
Preciado, J. A., 28, 34
Prior schooling, 16–17, 19–20, 25,
        28–29
Procedures, for student learning, 28–29, 41
Process, differentiated instruction and, 48,
        49–50
Product, differentiated instruction and, 48,
        49–50
Professional development, 132–137,
        145–146
Pull-out lessons, 19, 26n2
Putman, S. M., 6, 28

Question types, learning differences and, 33

Rafferty, L. A., 29
Rainbolt, S., 36
Ramirez, P. C., 46
Rasooli, A., 77
Readiness, differentiation and, 48–49
Receptive/productive language use, 66–68,
        144
Reflection/Reflective questions, on core
        practices, 138
    assessment, 93
    building positive learning environment, 42
    content and language instruction, 60
    knowing students, 26
    language and literacy development, 75
    relationship-building and advocacy, 110
Refugees, traumatic experiences among, 34–35
Relationship-building (core practice)
    among stakeholders, 94–95
    classroom examples, 106–109
    dimensions of, 96–106
    teaching techniques/methods/resources,
        109–110, 146
Restorative justice circles, 36
Reyes, R., 46
Roos, P. D., 103
Rosa, J., 26n1
Rose, D., 69
Routines, for student learning, 28–29, 41
Rubrics, creating and using, 91, 145
Rueda, R., 47

Saito, K., 44
Salazar, M., 1, 5, 6, 46
Sanford, A. K., 28, 34
Santamaría, L. J., 50
Santiago-Negrón, N., 103, 104
Saunders, W. M., 66
Scaffolding, 46–47, 59, 142
    differentiation and, 48
Schmitt, N., 63
Schneeberg, A., 62
Scullin, B. L., 66
Self-advocacy, 130–131
Self-assessment, 81
Self-care, for teachers, 109–110, 145
Shanahan, T. E., 15
Short, D., 51
Siegel, M. A., 77
Siwatu, K. O., 6, 28
Sleeter, C., 1
Snow, C. E., 15
Snowberg, K. E., 105

Social-emotional learning (SEL)
    cultural adaptations/expectations and, 34
    multi-tiered support for, 35–36
    skills development strategies, 33–36,
        41–42
Souto-Manning, M., 4, 7, 13
Spatzer, A., 44, 47–48
Spilt, J. L., 13
Stallworth, C., 4
Standardized assessments, 77, 132
    interpreting, 81–82
Starker-Glass, T. V., 6, 28
Stein, H., 98
Stephanie (elementary ESOL teacher),
    knowing students classroom practice
        example, 20–22
Stierer, B., 44
Stillman, J., 4
Stress, time constraints and, 128–129
Stroupe, D., 2
Student abilities, building on existing, 32–33
Student experience/knowledge
    differentiation and, 48
    humanizing pedagogy and, 6
    inferencing activity and, 21–22
    teacher understanding of, 17–18
Student interests
    differentiation and, 49
    teacher understanding of, 17–18, 19–20, 25
Students with limited or interrupted formal
        education (SLIFE), 16–17, 28–29
Stump, M., viii
Summative (formal) assessment, 76, 145
    designing and using, 78–81
    interpreting, 81–82
Sustaining pedagogy (cultural and linguistic),
    viii, 30–33
Swain, M., 66

Talking circles, proactive/responsive, 36
TC (secondary ESOL teacher), 76
    content and language instruction example,
        53–57
    knowing students example, 22–25
    language and literacy development
        example, 70–72
Teachers. See Classroom teachers
Teaching context/experience, humanizing
    practice in. See Humanizing pedagogy/
    practice
TeachingWorks, 2
Teemant, A., 4
Tenore, F. B., 28, 29

Thijs, J. T., 13
Thomas, S., 34
Thomas, W. P., 64
Thompson, J., 2, 100
Tienda, M., 34
Tigert, J., viii
Time constraints, 128–131
Tomlinson, C. A., 44, 47, 48, 49
Tong, V., 34
Translanguaging, 31–32, 142
Trauma-informed teaching, 34–36
Turkan, S., 69, 83

Uchihara, T., 63

Vadasy, P. F., 15
Valdés, G., 64
VanPatten, B., 44
Varghese, M., 4
Venn diagrams, 20
Villegas, A. M., 30
Visible criteria, in authentic assessment, 81
Vocabulary
    development of, supportive strategies for,
        62–64, 143–144
    language demands and, 51
Vygotsky, L. S., 46

Walqui, A., 66
"Warm demander," 29–30
Webb, K., 64, 65
Webb, S., 63
Wei, L., vii
Welner, K. G., 4
WestEd, 17
Whitaker, M. C., 28, 29
Whitford, D. K., 77
WIDA ACCESS, 17, 82, 92, 145
Wiggins, G., 79
Wiliam, D., 76
Windschitl, M., 2
Wong, S., 61
Wright, W. E., 64, 101, 104
Wubbels, T., 13

Xu, Y., 77

Yanagisawa, A., 63
Young, E., 4

Zandi, H., 77
Zavala, M., 1
Zong, J., 16

About the Authors

Megan Madigan Peercy is a professor in the Applied Linguistics and Language Education and the Teacher Education and Professional Development programs at the University of Maryland, where she also serves as an associate dean in the College of Education. Her research focuses on pedagogies of teacher education; the development of teacher educators; and the preparation and development of teachers throughout their careers, as they work with linguistically and culturally diverse learners. She has taught ESOL and Spanish to students from preschool to adults.

Johanna M. Tigert is associate professor of Curriculum and Instruction in the School of Education at University of Massachusetts Lowell. Her research focuses on the teaching and learning of multilingual students across informal and formal educational contexts. Dr. Tigert has taught ESOL to multilingual students from preschool to community college.

Daisy E. Fredricks is an assistant professor of Teaching and Learning and the Director of Teacher Education at Grand Valley State University. Her research focuses on instructional practices that teachers use with multilingual learners and how learners respond to such practices. She is a former elementary and middle school ESL and Spanish teacher and has taught ESL to adult multilingual learners.

About the Authors